Discipline and Morale in School and College

By the same author

Time and its Importance in Modern Thought
(Methuen, 1937; reissued Russell & Russell, New York, 1970)

Psychology in the Service of the School
(Methuen, 1951; reprinted 1961)

The Slow Learner
(Methuen, 1957; Second Edition and Paperback, 1968)

Teaching the Slow Learner, Vol. I: *In the Special School*;
Vol. II: *In the Primary School*; Vol. III: *In the Secondary School*
(Editor) (Methuen, 1961)

Educating Older People
(Tavistock, 1962; Second Edition, Social Science Paperback, 1970)

Discipline and Morale
in School and College

A STUDY OF GROUP FEELING

M. F. Cleugh

TAVISTOCK PUBLICATIONS

First published in 1971
By Tavistock Publications Limited
11 New Fetter Lane,
London EC4

Printed in Great Britain
In 12 on 13 point Bembo
By Cox & Wyman Ltd, Fakenham, Norfolk

SBN 422 73730 5

To K. L. H.

Contents

Contents

Acknowledgements

I am glad to take this opportunity of thanking all those who have helped me with this book. Colleagues, friends, and students have given me the benefit of their knowledge and common sense in countless discussions, and allowed me to use their experiences in the case studies. I am particularly grateful to Dr T. R. Batten, Miss H. M. Devereux, Miss K. L. Hanks, and Mrs M. A. Redmond, who all read the book in manuscript, and were unstintingly helpful. I am indebted to 'Miss Read' and Messrs Michael Joseph for permission to include extracts from *Village School*. Finally I would like to thank my splendid secretary, Mrs I. Clason, for all her help.

M. F. Cleugh
Whittington, Salop.

Part One · Case Studies

Introduction

For a long time I have been concerned with a nexus of related ideas: group spirit, morale, discipline, discrimination, stigma. How are these connected with leadership, both that of the assigned person in authority, lecturer or teacher, and that of the dominant spirits within the group? What is their relation to backwardness, and the place of the slow learner in the school morale system? Where does streaming fit in? How can a good group spirit assist what I have elsewhere (Cleugh, 1962, Chapter 2) called 'social learning' and by what mechanisms does it operate? What part do good communications play in the development and maintenance of good morale? What about the morale of teachers themselves, as distinct from that of their pupils? These questions are basic, and they overlap and subdivide in a most perplexing manner. No sooner does one catch on to one question than it turns into another. It seems to me that a study of morale, which has been surprisingly little considered in educational literature, occupies a key position in this imbroglio. It is a more useful topic to study than discipline, which rapidly tends to degenerate into a consideration of punishment, and corporal punishment at that, and once that Gorgon's head has been raised one can say goodbye to any rational discussion while the proponents and opponents argue hotly and emotionally. Meanwhile common sense and rationality fly out of the window and wider issues are forgotten. By contrast, the study of morale is a useful aspect to approach the Gorgon's head – from the back, so to speak – for in the last resort one cannot have good discipline without good morale. How can a helpful group feeling, an accepting climate which gives individuals a chance to grow and encourages social learning, be fostered? We are still in the stage of needing detailed factual data before we can proceed, on which hypotheses can be built.

The plan of this book, therefore, is simple. In the first part are a number of case studies and examples of varying degrees of complexity. Some are described in detail, others are much briefer and exemplify a single point. Some are followed by comments on the main issues involved, and these it is hoped will act as pointers or guides for the discussion of problems which takes up the second half of the book. With the exception of the fictionalized 'Village School' the examples are genuine, but obviously steps have been taken to prevent identification, and names and other details have been changed, so that any similarity of names is purely coincidental, and no reference to any individual living or dead is intended. We need constantly to remind ourselves that the stuff of education is nearer to the classroom, in all its complexities, than to the library with its neat psychological and sociological abstractions and classifications, which can quickly become barren if not constantly tested against actual cases and situations. I begin with a longish case which studies a group from its beginning to its end.

1 *The Joint Fieldwork Exercise*

In this case study I propose to describe a group which lasted for two weeks, examining particularly the interrelationships which developed between staff and students, the effectiveness or otherwise of its leadership, and the consequence of these on the development of group morale.

Much of the detail may sound trivial, but it is not just gossip. Through incidents a picture of the whole situation is built up, and without them the analytical discussion that follows would be meaningless.

The situation is seen through the eyes of an observer, Miss Oakes, who made fairly full written notes each evening, and these form the basis of the description below. She said that she tried to be as honest and objective as she could, and to make it clear which were factual statements of events and which were her own gloss on those events.

Two colleges, Thames and Clyde, decided to run a joint field exercise. The leader, Mr May, and nine students, three men and six women, came from Thames. The deputy leader, Miss Lane, two other staff members, Mrs Carter and Miss Oakes, and nine students, one man and eight women, came from Clyde. In addition there was an Australian couple, Mr and Mrs French, with their twelve-year-old son John. The Frenches could not be classed as either students or staff (Mr French was doing postgraduate work at Clyde), and because of their age they tended to occupy an intermediate position. Three of the Clyde students, Miss Cullen, Miss Watt, and Miss Wooler, were from Miss Lane's personal tutorial group: the other members of staff had had no previous ties with the students, except for Miss Oakes, who knew Mr French.

The following brief notes give Miss Oakes's impressions of the student members as they first appeared to her, and then on closer acquaintanceship.

Miss Allen	(Thames)	dim	dim
Miss Bates	T	giggly	flighty
Miss Bell	(Clyde)	(not identified)	unstable
Miss Bower	T	steady	good ability, stubborn
Miss Carr	T	rather weak	pleasant
Miss Cullen	C	flighty	and how!
Miss Day	C	quite good	quite good
Mr Elias	T	unstable	nice, *not* unstable
Mr Gill	T	good	plausible
Miss James	T	unstable	able but unstable
Miss Lay	T	unstable	giggly
Miss Ling	C	quite good	quite good, obstinate
Miss Mill	C	good	weak when difficulties arise
Mr Richards	T	good	not bad, can be obstinate
Mr Singh	C	quiet, able	quiet, able
Miss Taylor	C	unstable	a real problem
Miss Watt	C	(not identified)	quiet, pleasant
Miss Wooler	C	harmless	good type

Mr Elias and Mr Singh came from overseas, as did Miss Mill. Apart from Mr Gill, who was in his mid-twenties, the other students were all round about twenty-one. Mr May and Mrs Carter were about fifty, Miss Lane and Miss Oakes in their late thirties.

The day-by-day account of events appears on the following pages, with the comments set out opposite for ease of reference.

Description of events

1. *1st day.* It was evident (noted Miss Oakes) that Miss Lane and Mrs Carter distrust Mr May. He is facetious – played for popularity by making students giggle in train. Some of the things he says are inaccurate.
2. Mrs Carter comments that the students seem to be a weak group, but Miss Lane disagrees. Mr Elias remarks that the group seems pretty dull. Miss Oakes also finds them unpromising. Mr May is extremely desirous for the fortnight to be successful.
3. Mr May and Miss Lane indulge in backbiting and express a good deal of hostility to various absent notabilities.
   Very woolly opening talks by both Lane and May.
4. Pairing of Thames and Clyde students for field tasks done by Lane without consulting them, but she dropped an earlier idea she had of compulsorily fixing the rooming lists.

5. *2nd day.* Lane and Carter sat together at the top of the table for breakfast and dinner, but they did split at supper – Lane seemed very self-conscious about her place at the top. May rebuked the students at lunch – not their fault, bad instructions. Lane and Carter also dissatisfied with students. May and Lane expressed hostility again towards (absent) organizer.
6. Doubt about validity of May's instructions – hesitation. The students said among themselves, 'You can't believe him.' Very weak questions from students – not checked by May in chair – others very bored. The three Clyde staff felt May's leadership was much to blame – in particular, as he was not resident with the others.
7. Some silly byplay among the students of the 'We're better than you' type was definitely encouraged by Lane.

8. Oakes talked to most of the students in turn and found them quite nice as individuals. She found herself increasingly irritated by Lane who needed to be the non-stop centre of attention, very ostentatiously in charge. It was at this point that she

Comments

1. An unsatisfactory situation to begin with.

2. *Was* this in fact a particularly weak group of students? Much of the unsatisfactory behaviour later may be reaction to poor leadership, but it is noteworthy that three out of four first impressions (including a student's) were doubtful. There seem to be more marked 'unstable' than one would normally expect.

3. It looks as if the only common ground between the two leaders is their joint readiness to indulge in unpleasant gossip.

4. Highhanded actions rarely gain cooperation.

5. Emphasizing their separateness rather than trying to set a good example by mixing.

6. The unwisdom of facetious behaviour is now coming home to roost. When he means what he says he is not believed.

7. Also an unwise move. In a situation which starts off with two camps the very last thing that leaders should be doing is to encourage a competitive element to creep in.

8. This is a common finding, that individual members often give a better impression than the group as a whole.

decided to make a study of the group interactions, and found that writing notes relieved her feelings!

3rd day. Students varied in ability on their fieldwork – some just drifted. Oakes queried dim student (Cullen) but Lane said she was one of her best. Lane poor at thanking helpful visitors and May departed for the day at 10.30 a.m.

9. One of the effects of lack of trust in the leaders is that it raises doubts whether adequate briefing has been given to outside helpers. Carter and Lane sat at the top of the table for all meals.

10. In the evening they treated two students (the acceptable Richards and Cullen who was one of Lane's own students) to a drink, while completely ignoring the rest. This seemed unwise. The students talk to Oakes pleasantly.

11. Lane ticked off students who asked for sandwiches – students annoyed (they had not been told beforehand of procedure re absence from meals). Lane then had to smooth hostel down. Students also complained of cost. Another grumbling session by Lane and Carter. French bought coffee for the staff. When Lane grizzled, French asked if she was anxious about the success of the fortnight, but she denied this. Today was said to be better than yesterday – actually the group was a bit easier – some talk across the table mainly started by French and Oakes. Frenches are a great social cement and the child is a help too.

4th day. More trouble with insufficient instructions – Lane dressed down Cullen, who is usually a favourite.

12. May handled the fieldwork better – the group kept together and were punctual – Lane firm about this. Visiting expert gave good guidance, but students not properly informed until supper who he was. He was nicely thanked by Lane. Lane critical of John French, wandering about on his own during the fieldwork. Students properly consulted re choice of day's programme by Lane – this went better.

13. More grizzling in evening at behaviour of students by Lane and Carter – two examples of their impertinence to her given by Lane (a) over sandwiches yesterday, (b) asked by her not to

9. Again doubt and uncertainty.

10. Any suspicion of favouritism is the most obvious of all pitfalls to be avoided.

11. Again failure to give clear instructions *before* trouble arises leads to bad feelings.

12. Improved leadership, improved response.

13. Blame is projected outwards on to the students who are 'impertinent' – no apparent readiness to consider how she herself had been to blame. Lack of respect evident.

rush up for second helpings they had said, 'What business is it of yours?'

14. Meantime the cliques are solidifying – only Gill and Cullen of the students are 'in', the rest are 'out'. The only ones who try general talk across the table are the Frenches again and Oakes. The absence of May and the immaturity of Lane means little effective leadership.

15. Rumours get around before there is official intimation – several times there has been no information and then a blow-up because students have done the wrong thing. Altercations with students undignified.

5th day. It has now got to open cheek – Lane angrily reported conversation, 'It's got nothing to do with you what we do.' To which she replied, 'If you don't fit in with the party you can leave it.'

16. Carter said certain women students take advantage because Lane is young, but that this is an advantage with the men! Party drifted lackadaisically through its fieldwork. French rallied the party by singing. Lane took charge well when a student fainted. May's instructions to group contained inaccuracy which Oakes tried to correct. Rest of party kept waiting while four staff were taken off to drink.

17. At the tea pause, Lane made efforts to invite Watt and Wooler (both her own students) to join the staff. No attempt at mixing with the others.

18. Later she called to them saying, 'Be ill tomorrow so that I can get off fieldwork.' At supper, May exhorted the students – 'Be matey, praise everything, and above all drink!' – and praised them fulsomely.

19. The students had taken the head of the table, and Lane and Carter were forced to split.

6th day. Carter and Oakes discussed differences in direction – May praising, Lane blaming. Reception – speeches by May and James. Lane – undignified laughter at lunch and posture at reception. Students said she drank a lot – much

14. Favouritism getting worse.

15. See 11.

16. Is this in fact the real reason? It becomes a *reductio ad absurdum* if no one under forty is 'old enough' to lead a party – however would we staff our schools and colleges? With more than ten years' gap between her and the oldest of the students, Miss Lane should have had plenty of leeway in her favour – had she behaved in a less immature and more integrative fashion.

17. Again disintegrative actions from the very one who should be trying to encourage unity within the group.

18. An extraordinary gaffe. Apart from its childishness, what are its repercussions likely to be on students' attitudes to the importance of the work they are supposed to be doing?

19. This counter-attack was to be expected sooner or later.

repartee. Christian names among students now, but very cliquey.

20. Oakes sat with James and Co. at lunch and told Lane this – thanked for doing it (James and Co. are thought to be outside the pale). Carter: 'I think *I'll* have to do some slumming.') Oakes: 'It wouldn't be a bad idea.' Query – does Carter feel Lane needs support? – she probably *could* help more by mixing with students. Students fairly responsible in talking to outsiders. May on return journey very relieved and self-congratulatory that critical day had passed off so well. Carter and Lane have discussed May and the background of altercation with French – got the reply, 'There is a lot more in leading a party than I had grasped.' Diplomatic, and ambiguous. Carter spoke to Oakes of May's insecurity and need to show off and cover up – apparently no realization that the same is also true of Lane.

7th day. May now less sure that yesterday was a success. Lane, Carter, and Oakes left party, agreeing to be back by 11 a.m. Oakes was back but others missing and May went without them at 11.10. At lunchtime, apologies – said they had phoned at this time, but no message came.

21. In the meantime, James showed sense – held party back from vanishing when bus stopped, with the official leaders missing, May presumably at the office, Lane goodness knows where.

22. Lane explained to Richards that she thought his speech yesterday much better than that of James. Lane ordered John to back of bus, John argued, Lane insisted, and finally John went but only just – not well handled. Another reception today, in the early evening – leading parts taken by Gill, Richards, and James. Much giggling. May mixed well, remainder of staff less well. Lane critical of French for not drinking.

23. The whole party (except May) returned to its quarters one hour late. Oakes asked James to give an apologetic explanation to the management, which she did. No other apologies were forthcoming.

20. An instructive incident, especially Mrs Carter's words. The lack of respect for the students is evident. Mrs Carter could have been a big help to a weak leader if instead of trying to prop her up, she *had* done more moving around – though, again, if she had done it in a 'slumming' way, she might have achieved little.

21. Students – even despised ones – can do more than they are given credit for.

22. Utterly unwise. Its only effect can have been divisive. It is contemptible to attempt to curry favour with one student by such obvious flattery at the expense of another.

23. General lack of consideration here.

24. Oakes invited James and Wooler, who happened to be handy, to go with her and help in the kitchen afterwards and this they did very pleasantly.

8th day. Lane ordered John about quite rudely – does she feel insecure even with a twelve-year-old? At lunch, the four staff together, and tensions coming to the surface. Much jockeying for position and taunting, e.g. May teasing Carter with rude remarks about Royal Family. Later Carter told Oakes how much she disliked May, would complain to her Principal back in Clyde, etc. May found an interest which he had in common with Oakes – probably more to annoy Lane and Carter than to please Oakes!

The afternoon's fieldwork badly overran its time, and Lane and Carter were furious as visitors were expected at the evening meal. (This was purely Lane's arrangement and no concern of May's.) Lane and May open altercation in front of the students, with Oakes trying to calm it down. May phoned hostel and explained everyone would be late.

25. Lane was more concerned to blame May than to retrieve the situation. (In the event, no visitors came.) After this fuss, May told students tall stories about his wartime exploits. Carter (to Oakes) named three students (all Thames) as tarts, omitting the (Clyde) one whom Oakes privately thought the worst, and named two Clyde girls and Gill and Richards as helpful – hardly an objective choice.

26. Later she said Thames and Clyde were not mixing well! (but Richards had commented they were mixing better).

At dinner, Lane ordered Oakes and the Frenches quite rudely to move to empty seats left at the top of the table. She later explained that this was because the local paper's photographer was expected!

27. The in-group and out-group are now very marked – only three students (Cullen, Gill, Richards) go anywhere near her, and they are rather familiar in manner.

9th day. Adult squabbles take first place today – students in

24. A positive approach to the students again brings forth a positive response. It is interesting that one of the students was from Clyde, the other from Thames. This is almost the only incident we hear of a definite staff attempt at integrating and this was largely accidental.

25. It is easier to blame other people than to do something constructive.

26. Failure to mix is not really surprising and can hardly be blamed on the students.

27. Chickens coming home to roost.

background. Inaccurate explanation by May to students. Lane criticized May openly to French. May now turning to attack Oakes for no obvious reason, and Lane and Carter very anxious to pass on to her all he said about her.

28. Lane openly bored on official visit and said so to her little group of student hangers-on. At dinner, empty space left as usual round Lane, and Carter moved at Lane's request back to her usual place at top. Carter reported that May blew off to the students re hitch-hiking – great fuss and deadlock at end. Oakes much less irritated by May than are Carter and Lane.

10th day
Examples of staff-student relationships
A. Lane went to fetch Bates, who said, 'It doesn't matter to you whether I come or not.' Lane: 'You are keeping twenty-four people waiting.' Bates: 'I don't care.'
B. Next she ticked off Bell and John for dancing in the street. Bell apologized later.
C. Richards (usually well in favour) was hanging back and she rebuked him. He replied, 'I don't see that it matters what I do. We weren't told that we were expected to keep up with the party. Anyway, if I did get left I could always hitch-hike back' – which was pretty insolent, in view of yesterday's fuss.

29. *D.* James to Carter: '*Must* you sit there? We were going to,' and flounces off elsewhere. Lane and Carter had for once left the head of the table to the students and their guests (it was a party) and sat in the middle with Oakes.

30. *E.* Lane to Lay and Mill, who were giggling, 'Either you behave yourselves or you leave this room.'

Staff-staff relations
May said: 'I've enjoyed talking to you people in turn, have learnt a lot. We must keep in touch.' This offended Lane and Carter. Carter: 'I've noticed you've tried to pick our brains' – – rather a drastic reply. Oakes thought that he seemed quieter and more honest. Lane fetched hot water for Carter and Oakes as well as herself. Carter spent the afternoon off on her own.

28. Again unwise familiarity – of the wrong sort – to students.

29. It seems incredible that a student should speak like this – but she did.

30. It seems even more incredible that these words and this tone were addressed, not to children of ten, but to grown women. It is to be remembered that Lane's own behaviour, at a previous reception, had been as unsuitable and undignified as theirs, so is it to be wondered at that this remark, which would have been shattering had respect been behind it, aroused nothing except resentment?

11th day. May still very quiet. Twice tried to argue with Oakes – really very rude and quite confused. Again said must keep in touch. May complimented the students at lunch on their excellent behaviour, coming after Lane, who had been curt. May afterwards tried to get Lane to agree they had behaved well, but she hedged. May said goodbye, as he was now returning to Thames. Few people at fieldwork – feeling of fizzling out.

31. Carter asked students to hurry with evening meal and they responded. She was pleased. French spoke to students re trip tomorrow. Both of them handled them better than Lane.

12th day. A free day. Very few in for supper. Gill suggested that coffees should come from the common fund, but Lane refused. Oakes ordered for herself and her two colleagues.

32. Gill and Cullen tagged on and Carter ordered two more coffees. The division between approved and non-approved students becomes ever more glaring. Oakes furious at this incident – wondered whether common funds had been used for this before.

13th day. Lane rebuked John for hanging on to Singh, and altercation with students re tipping. Gill joined the three women staff at lunch and cadged a drink from Lane. Gill and Cullen were also given tea at teatime. Lane paid for this and for their coffee – it seems fairly certain that the common fund is being used. Lane and Gill discussed the sheeplike qualities of the students at lunch – not wise.

33. After supper, Gill came to Lane objecting to the 11 p.m. rule of the hostel and expecting an exception to be made for him. Lane refused to intercede.

14th day. Oakes in charge of party. Had to quieten Lay (screaming in street). No further trouble. Richards got across hostel warden – latter full of complaints. Lane very curt with Richards – also said he had cheeked Carter. Lane helpful to sick student.

31. In spite of all that has gone before there is still a response to a positive approach.

32. More favouritism.

33. 'One law for the rich, another for the poor' – luckily it didn't come off this time.

34. Place very quiet – some have left, others writing up reports. Lane discussing her colleagues back at Clyde with a student.

35. *15th day*. Lane said it didn't matter how late Gill and Cullen were in to breakfast as they were in favour with hostel warden. Lane helpful to Singh who got into difficulty with baggage and stayed behind with him. Rest departed.

36. On journey back, James and Bower showed sense of responsibility – interesting that it should be those two as they had been in black books most of the time.

What a lot of tittle-tattle it all sounds! Yet this is the very stuff of interaction, and we shall get nowhere if we remain at the stage of enunciating virtuous generalities, remote from the muddle and the complexity of any group meetings. What is wanted is actual examples with details of interactions which we can then analyse and from which we can extract general ideas.

34. Ending not with a bang but with a whimper. As no feeling of group solidarity had been evoked, there was less feeling of regret at this fizzling-out of an ending.
35. Or did it? – see 33.

36. One can contrast their sense of responsibility with the irresponsibility of the favoured Gill.

Having commented briefly on separate incidents, I turn now to consider how these can be put together to make a diagnostic picture.

Discussion

First, let us start with a simple quantitative analysis by counting the number of positive actions and of negative actions reported. The length of each column tells its own story. Note, these are factual incidents: they are not dependent on Miss Oakes's interpretations, except that Miss Oakes provided the sampling out of the totality of all experiences, and we must therefore rely on her not having selected a biased sample.

Mr May *Positive*	*Negative*
Really wants success	Plays for popularity
	Inaccurate statements
	Backbiting and gossip
	Rebuking students unfairly
	Woolly instructions
	Hostile remarks about organizer
	Students disbelieve him
	Weak chairman
	Distrusted by three Clyde staff
	Missing after mid-morning
Handled fieldwork better	Ineffective leadership
	Rumours before instructions
	Careless and inaccurate instructions (repeatedly)
Usually praises	Fulsome praise
Becomes more realistic after being over-optimistic	Teasing Carter
Took positive action re visitors	Argument with Lane before everybody
	Boasting about war deeds
Positive approach to colleagues (rejected)	Attacks Oakes
	Fuss re hitch-hiking

May Positive	Negative
Oakes feels he is more honest	Arguing, rude and confused
Total 7	*Total 20* (not counting repetitions of 1 item)

The tabulation shows clearly the negative balance. On the whole his faults are omissions – failure to inspire trust or respect, ineffectiveness – rather than actual sins he committed.

Lane Positive	Negative
	Distrusts May
	Backbiting and gossip
	Woolly instructions
Dropped idea of compulsory rooming	Pairing without consulting
	Apartheid at table (repeated)
Thinks group not weak	Soon becomes dissatisfied
	Hostile remarks about organizer
	Encouraged silly competitiveness
	Need to be centre of attention
Thanked expert nicely	Ungracious thanks
	Favouritism (repeatedly)
	Rebuking students unfairly
	Grumbling session
	Too defensive to admit she wants success
	Criticized child
	Grumbling about students (repeatedly)
	Target for impertinence (repeatedly)
Consulted students re day's programme	Rumours before instructions

Lane Positive   *Negative*

Took charge well when student fainted	Immaturity taken advantage of
	Suggested students should malinger
	Usually blames
	Undignified behaviour
	Overdrinking
	Discussed May with French
Firm about students' punctuality	Unpunctual herself
	Flattering Richards at James's expense
	Trouble with John (repeatedly)
	No apologies for lateness of party
	Argument with May before everyone
	Did nothing herself to retrieve visitors
	Rude orders to Oakes and Frenches
	Openly bored and told students so
Fetched hot water for her colleagues	Threatening students
	Altercation re tipping
Refused misuse of common fund	Probably misuse of common fund
Refused exception to be made for Gill	Discussed other student with Gill
Helpful to sick student	Discussed her Clyde colleagues with student

Lane Positive	Negative
Helpful with luggage	Curt with Richards
Total 11	Total 38 (not counting numerous repetitions of 5 items)

When tabulated like this, it is interesting to see that the positive items are those where practical action has to be taken – sickness, luggage, hot water – and the negative items are overwhelmingly in her relationships with people. Every time her failure is one of sensitivity and imaginative thoughtfulness for others and their feelings. Again, the tabulated summary of episodes shows an overwhelmingly negative skew.

It would be unduly complicated and repetitive to continue similar balance sheets for all the other persons involved. It will be more profitable to turn now to discuss the issues that crop up repeatedly – undue bossiness of manner, rudeness, favouritism, apartheid, personal insecurity – and make notes on each of them.

1. *Authoritarianism.* Not surprisingly, our example shows the consistently unfavourable reactions evoked by undue bossiness of manner. The effects are even worse when authoritarianism is linked, as it often is here, with vagueness, inefficiency, and failure to give necessary information in good time. The resulting muddles are then blamed *in toto* on the students, who become convenient scapegoats for their elders' failures. Naturally this arouses resentment and a vicious circle is set up, with the high-handed actions and words of the leaders ever adding more fuel to the flames. These issue in:

2. *Rudeness.* Many people will read the account with astonishment: Can the students really have behaved like this? and, more incredulously: Can the staff really have spoken in this way? I do not know how typical or untypical this group's experience was – there is such a shortage of detailed accounts of actual group behaviour available that it is not possible to say. One's impression is that since everybody seemed to take the proceedings very much

for granted it is not as untypical as it ought to be. In any case, it did occur. Certainly recent accounts of widespread resentment among students in many different institutions leave no one with any feeling of complacency. Let us take it as axiomatic that those who speak rudely to students, and show by their actions that they despise them, are likely to meet with as much cheek as Miss Lane did.

3. *Favouritism.* One of the most elementary maxims of the teacher at any stage of learning is the need to avoid favouritism, and it is indeed surprising to see it so rampant at a very high stage of the educational ladder. The staff concerned were presumably highly qualified compared with teachers in general and yet the most glaring differentiations seem to have been practised continually in this instance. The division into in-group and out-group apart from its blatant unfairness is one obvious source for poor student morale.

4. *Apartheid* poses a more tricky problem. There is a sense in which authority does bring apartness and in which it is right that it should. But the attempt to cling on to the outward trappings of authority – a special seat, a special gown – has its ludicrous side. Especially is this so where, as in this example, the proper functions of authority are not well carried out and where, again as in this example, the exercise of apartheid is linked with an unsuitable and unwise familiarity – discussion of students and colleagues with students, undue mateyness, and so on. This leads to the final point:

5. *Personal insecurity.* It is the insecure individual who needs to take refuge in outward show, who fluctuates between unsuitable friendliness and dictatorial aloofness, who must be propped up by a clique of favourites, whose own lack of basic respect for himself makes him ever ready to take refuge in tattling and backbiting. We have two prime specimens here. In a sense, it is personal insecurity that lies at the back of all the previous points. That being so, how is it to be helped? In any case it is deeply disturbing

that power and leadership should be vested in individuals as immature and insecure as these.

A Speculative Exercise

In the light of the foregoing, let us try to imagine a very different story, how Mr May and his colleagues *could* have acted if they had tried throughout to achieve a pleasant group atmosphere, with particular reference to the relationships between staff and students: or, if it is too unrealistic to posit a universal change of heart, how the leader alone could have acted differently. Let us grant that they started off under difficulties. They didn't know each other very well to begin with and what they did know they didn't find especially congenial. The students were rather a scratch lot, the balance of men and women was poor, and they too came from two camps. In these circumstances the paramount importance of sinking all difference and trying to get a good working relationship going should be the main objective of the staff. The difficulties were there but they should not have been insuperable. When we think of all the other situations in education at the present time which demand mergers – youth camps, the amalgamation of schools in comprehensivization – the problem is a vital one and means must be found of solving it. Our little example has many parallels in wider educational fields.

1st day. The staff met, and metaphorically walked round each other like dogs. They didn't like each other any better at first impression in this imagined story than in the real one, but they were each more circumspect in their conversation, because Mr Hay as the senior, took the lead in discouraging any attempts of the others to find an easy consensus by criticizing their principals. He thought ruefully, 'If I encourage them to reject authority, why should they respect mine?' At the same time he was particularly careful not to present an authoritarian approach, though he tried to have a businesslike meeting and to allocate responsibilities clearly among his staff. He noted that Miss Lane was inclined to be bossy, Mrs Carter to fuss, and Miss Oakes to withdraw and wash her hands of the whole thing, and he decided as far as possible to play down these weaknesses. Miss Lane was clearly better at dealing with things than with people, and her efficiency and hard work could be put to good advantage. Though fussy and gossipy, Mrs Carter meant well and would run round endlessly if directed. Miss Oakes had a nice attitude to people, and could be given more to do. He regretted more than ever that it was absolutely impossible for him to live in hostel with the party – if this had not been so he would have sacrificed his previous plans to live out, having seen his lieutenants – and he decided to be present himself as early and as late as he could, and leave little to chance.

When he spoke to the students he made no attempt to play for popularity. His manner was simple, direct, and friendly. He gave information clearly and fully. He asked for questions and dealt with them courteously. He then handed the meeting over to Miss Lane, for her domestic instructions. She began rather aggressively, 'The following students *will* do so and so', and as she finished the first list he added quietly, 'Let me just explain. We don't know each other yet, and we thought it might be a good idea to mix Thames and Clyde, so that we all take pot-luck together. I'm sure you'll agree.' Incipient belligerence, sulkiness, and fearfulness were thus allayed, at least to some extent. The students' common sense told them the idea was good and they'd give it a try. Mr Hay wondered whether to end the evening with a let-us-each-introduce-ourselves session, but since there seemed to be rather a large number of shy, nervous-looking individuals to whom it might be more of a strain than a help, he gave up the idea.

2nd day. By the end of the morning the *ad hoc* student pairing seemed to be shaking down – some stresses and strains were evident, but there were also some good mixes, for example Mr Gill and Miss Cullen. At lunch time, Mr Hay was sorry to see that Miss Lane and Mrs Carter were resolutely heading the table, and he resolved to drop a hint, in the first instance to Mrs Carter. He himself sat in the middle of the students, as did Miss Oakes, and tried to get general conversation going. As might be expected, the students sat in blocks of Clyde and Thames. He was tempted to order general post, but reflected that it was better to wait and let it come (with encouragement) rather than forcing an issue now. Some silly byplay among the students began – 'We're better than you' and he let it ride for a bit, until he saw that Miss Lane encouraged it. He then felt he had to intervene, saying equably 'We can forget all that for a fortnight. While we're here we're the Thames-Clyde express' – a poor joke, but enough to deflect the issue. His tone was more important than the actual words. He hoped that Miss Lane wouldn't think he'd let her down and went out of his way to re-establish her position by saying a minute or two later, 'Miss Lane and I have been thinking that . . .' Even if it was her own fault it was his job to rescue her (but not his job to allow the unsuitable badinage to continue). He gathered later that Miss Lane and Mrs Carter were dissatisfied with the students and, it was quite true, some of their questions *were* pretty weak, but, as chairman, he was able to control the meeting so that it did not drag on too long.

3rd day. Mr Hay had intended to leave half-way through the morning but he decided to stay because he felt that staff-student relationships could go either way. Although the students were pleasant with him and with Miss Oakes, he sensed a certain resentment and lack of trust in their attitude to Miss Lane – and he had to admit she asked for it. That crazy business of treating two students and ignoring the rest, for instance! At least he was glad to see that Mrs Carter had taken his hint and was prepared to circulate at meals – this was bound to end sooner or later in Miss Lane doing the same, and the mystique of apartheid would be broken. He was careful to see that *he* thanked the helpful visitors and that the students were adequately briefed as to their identity. He reminded Miss Lane to make sure the students knew procedure for absence from meals. He was sorry to see that some of the students had drifted through their fieldwork, but on the whole he thought morale was reasonably high, and was improving.

And so, to the 4th day.

There is no need to pursue this imaginary story further. Have I begged the question by changing Mr May into Mr Hay? The postulated changes in the leader's conduct raise the key issue – do people behave as they have to, or would they, given greater awareness, act differently once they realized the detrimental effect of their behaviour on the group? It would certainly have been pulling a fast one, in this imaginary story, to change for the better everyone, students and staff alike, so that all became sweetness and light. Quite unrealistic! But it could easily happen that one key individual acting differently could make resultant changes (gradually, not dramatically) in the reactions of the others, and, since the leader is the main determinant of morale in the group, it seemed best to choose him as the exemplar of change. The opposite view, that *all* act within circumscribed limits of their own natures, seems unduly deterministic – at least if the limits are very stringently set – and is disproved by the students' varying reactions. Granted they were not a specially satisfactory lot and granted that there would always be plenty of backsliding from them whatever the circumstances, there is abundant evidence from the real story that they were prepared to respond over and over again to a positive gesture. This was shown by their consistent friendliness and lack of rudeness to Miss Oakes, by their response to Mrs Carter when she appealed to them to hurry, by their repeated rising to any situation (21, 24, 36) where they were given responsibility.

So it is too simple to say, 'This is the sort of person he is and so he will always act in this way: it is his nature.' We have also to consider the group setting in which this man is placed. If it had been different, he might have appeared in a different light, and shown other facets of his character. Miss James, for instance, was a student who could appear intolerably rude and objectionable (see 29) and who for most of the fortnight was definitely 'agin the government,' yet she also appears on several occasions to possess many good qualities.

It is surely the duty of the leaders of any group to do their utmost to ensure that the group climate shall be favourable.

I conclude that this little example should be taken as an awful warning. It happened, and it happened unnecessarily. While things of this nature occur, and at a quite high educational level, what is the use of elaborate theoretical constructs *as long as they stay at a theoretical level and are not translated into action?* What we need is the detailed examination of actual case studies, whose results we then need to take to heart – and act upon.

*   *   *

This example was a useful one to begin with, because of its short time-span of two weeks. Usually events are spread over a much longer duration – school groups and classes usually last for a year, and in some schools the membership of a particular class may be very little changed over three or four years. It is more difficult to study the interplay of persons and events over a longer time, but it would be artificial if we kept only to untypical 'short courses' because of their greater simplicity and ease of handling.

Next let us look at two schools, similar in many respects, whose outlooks and ethos were quite different, and follow them over a period of time, one school year.

2 Two Contrasted Schools

Towne Secondary Modern School for Girls was one of the earliest in the country to enter the field of public examinations, at that time almost wholly thought of as the prerogative of grammar schools. Having achieved a good deal of success with its candidates at O-level, it began to set its sights higher and think in terms of retaining a handful of girls for A-levels, and was very proud of the one or two who had just left it to enter a College of Education. Because of this striving policy, it had gained a high reputation in the district: let us examine whether it was, in fact, the 'good school' it was reputed to be, in terms of the morale and happiness of the rank and file.

We will begin by considering the situation at the other extreme from the academic stars, the remove classes. There was a good deal of trouble here, and discipline was frankly bad, particularly in the Upper Remove which contained a difficult group of 3rd and 4th years, whose sights were set only on the day they would leave. Specialist teachers were glad when the one or two lessons they had each week with them were over, and there was an alarming turn-over in their 'class' teachers, who followed each other in quick succession to break down, to give up teaching, or to graduate to a less-exposed niche in the school. Finally, the head, with a very tempting enticement of a large allowance, appointed Mrs Hall and gave her a free hand. Mrs Hall was a middle-aged woman with long experience of junior and infant teaching, so that she was thoroughly conversant with methods of teaching the basic subjects, at a level lower than the usual 'general subjects' teacher in a secondary modern school can cope with. More important, she was a thoroughly stable, solid person with a genuine interest in, and non-sentimental compassion for, these girls, and was able to relate to them on a human person-to-person level. She threw out the arid English 'exercises' and the dull arithmetic, and adopted instead a primary-type activity approach, so that the girls were all working on an individualized programme, each at her own level. The *content* of their work was not babyish, but related to their adolescent interests in beauty, boys, babies, and home-making. Mrs Hall tried to foster a close link with the housecraft department. Unfortunately the particular housecraft teacher who taught these girls was strongly tinged with the common staff attitude towards them, and was not specially interested in them, but Mrs Hall saw to it that the girls came prepared for their practical lessons by centring much of their classroom work in English, spelling, and arithmetic (weighing and measuring) on their needs in these lessons. As she had less occasion to complain 'they can't make notes/spell/weigh/bring change' the housecraft teacher became more favourably disposed to them, and they on their part, feeling themselves less at a disadvantage in her lessons than they had done, reciprocated by causing less disturbance by their behaviour. As in fact several of them were reasonably capable in practical affairs, housecraft was a subject in which they could potentially approach more nearly to an average standard than they could in more academic work, and they began to feel success instead of the all-round failure that they had previously experienced. So their interests were tapped, they took more care and pride in their housecraft work than they had previously done, and the specialist began to feel they weren't so bad after all, and even to defend them on occasion in staff-room conversations. PE was another specialist subject where potentially many of the Remove could have gained a reasonable success, but here the story was less happy, mainly because coaching a gifted minority towards a high

standard of performance in school teams was the main concern of
the specialists, as we shall see later. To do them justice, they were
under pressure from the headmistress, who liked to be able to read
out at Prize Day an imposing list of County trophies won. So in
PE the rank and file (not to mention the troublemakers of Upper
Remove) took second place, and there was constant battle with
Upper Remove over malingerers, 'forgotten' kit, and generally
uncooperative behaviour. To some extent this improved under
Mrs Hall's influence but it would be fair to say that the opportunities for using PE as a medium of success and morale building for
these girls were not seized. The art specialist also was not particularly interested, and she was genuinely overpressed, owing to
the large demands on her time that were made by two senior girls
who were staying on to take A-level Art. Mrs Hall found it was
simpler to take her own art, and though this meant that some of
the wider opportunities of the art-room were not available for the
girls, at least under her eye they were behaving and concentrating
more than they had been in the habit of doing previously, so that
the supposed opportunities were never in fact taken. As time went
on, Mrs Hall, who had begun by having the usual battles and
disappointments with them, gradually began to win through, as
the girls responded both to her firmness and to her genuine
interest in them. They realized that she was on their side, and
though she would not stand any nonsense, she was sincerely trying
to help them to control themselves, so that they could find growing up more acceptable. As this was what in their hearts they
wanted to do, they gradually became more ready to conform to
the undemanding, but necessary limitations that Mrs Hall imposed. So a feeling of trust grew up between Mrs Hall and her
class: they relied on her to keep the ring, so that they were not left
entirely at the mercy of their wayward impulses and their immature and frequent quarrels. Her confidence in herself as a person
and in her own skill as a teacher was firm enough to withstand the
constant buffetings and the predictable backslidings that tested it.
It was by no means an easy victory, nor was it achieved without a
good deal of wear and tear on Mrs Hall, who often went home

exhausted, complaining that her twenty seniors were far more tiring than forty normal juniors. Gradually, however, a regime of peace and order was established during the (roughly) half of the week that her class was with her, and no longer did they rush out like demented beings at break to spread disorder round the school. So complaints of their general behaviour in corridors, dining-room, and playground became fewer, and, apart from one or two, they were less frequently in detention (or refusing to go). A sensi-tive index of their improved adjustment was their much better attendance, which no longer lagged so abysmally below that of the rest of the school.

In the Lower Remove, the situation was basically similar to that of the Upper Remove before Mrs Hall's arrival in that nobody was particularly concerned to defend them and many to decry them. They were the last considered when the timetable was made up, and in effect were taken in general subjects by whoever happened to be left over when the other forms had been slotted in. So they were expected to conform to the varying regimes of a number of teachers for which they were too immature without having the advantages of genuine specialist teaching. Their frag-mented timetable was much too elaborate for them to cope with and their bewilderment, forgetfulness, and unpunctuality were signs of this. Most children enter the secondary school with a feeling of a new start, and are ready in the first instance to try their best, but when they are faced with a confusing and impersonal situation beyond their level of maturity, after a time the efforts cease and they lapse into apathy. So it was not really a hopeful sign that Lower Remove were relatively quiet and conforming: they were merely another Upper Remove in the making. The older girls *appeared* a greater problem because they noisily and openly rejected the mores of the school, and caused the head and staff forcibly to notice them – hence the appointment of Mrs Hall. A more farsighted policy would have looked first on how these girls came to be as they were, and have given more consideration to the needs of the younger pupils.

Although the two Remove classes showed most sharply the

contrast with the impressive façade of examination and sports successes, difficulties were by no means confined to these two classes. In lesser degree, the same concomitants of poor morale were to be found in the C classes. In fact it was noteworthy that when Upper Remove settled down to some extent under Mrs Hall's influence, 3 and 4C became the major targets of staff grumbles. Towards the end of the school year, the head invited Mrs Hall to transfer across to become form mistress of 3C. Mrs Hall was not at all pleased at this compliment, for it showed clearly that the head had no understanding and no interest beyond plugging the most troublesome gaps. She tried to persuade the head that she was still needed by Upper Remove, but it was a blow to her own morale, for it was only too clear that the head regarded her merely as a portable discipline machine, with little consideration for the thought and care for the needs of the girls for steadiness and security that underlay what she was doing and provided its rationale.

It would be fair to say that the school showed a sort of schizophrenia – Dr Jekyll at the top, and Mr Hyde becoming increasingly evident the further down the school one went. The abler girls felt loyalty to the school and found it a stimulating place, but even in the B streams the rot was beginning to set in. It was two 3B girls, brilliant athletes, who refused to turn up to run for the school on a Saturday in the county championships. They had a good chance of winning, but they refused to bring this kudos to their school. (A similar situation was described in 'The Loneliness of the Long Distance Runner', but the boy there was a known delinquent at odds with society: it is disquieting that the same lack of involvement could be found in Towne, a most respectable establishment.) Too much must not be read into the behaviour of two disaffected adolescents, but it was a warning sign when taken in conjunction with the rest. On all objective tests (attendance, wearing of uniform, support of school functions, etc.), conformity to the ethos of the school decreased the further down the streams one went.

This is a fairly common finding, and by no means confined to Towne. Hargreaves (1967), for example, found the same in his closely documented study of a boys' secondary modern in Lancashire described in *Social Relations in a Secondary School*, and so did Jackson (1964) in *Streaming*. Both of them used this phenomenon as an argument against streaming, but for our purposes here it is sufficient to make the point that lack of commitment to the purposes of the school was widespread at Towne: the streaming question will be considered later.

I conclude that when disaffection shown in bad behaviour and apathy is *endemic* in a school, so that when one form ceases to be the focus of staff criticism another takes its place, there is little point in blaming troublesome individuals. It is more worth while to ask whether the curriculum and values of the school are suitable to meet the needs of the majority of its members. It is excellent that the abler children should be well catered for, and given vocational and developmental opportunities, but what about the rest? Low morale in a sizeable section of the school should always be a cause for serious self-examination among those responsible for its policies.

The story of Towne is a fairly familiar one (apart, unfortunately, from the role played in it by Mrs Hall) and raises some very pertinent questions. Was this, in fact, a 'good' school? Is the large-scale disaffection inevitable, or can it be avoided? Could the organization have been improved? Or did the problems go beyond the day-to-day running of the school and stem from the attitudes and values of the staff? What about the head's leadership?

Before discussing these issues, let us take another short example, also from a girls' secondary modern, of about the same size (roughly 100 per age-group) and also from a reasonably prosperous skilled-working-class area. In this school, which I will call Othertown, again the classes were streamed.

The general atmosphere of Othertown was lively and stimulating, but it lacked the striving quality of Towne. The head was anxious to provide opportunities for her abler girls, but she was also equally anxious to provide opportunities for successful achievement right down the school to the remove classes. The head's teaching timetable embraced all levels in the school – it was not so

D

much that she 'took her share' of teaching the backward classes (with its suggestion of a nasty medicine democratically endured), as that she enjoyed all her teaching, different though the content might be at different levels. She remarked that the childishness of the Lower Remove could be very appealing, and said they had preserved some of the freshness and zest of juniors, so she liked taking them. This attitude spread over to the other teachers and it was noticeable that much more positive comments about the less able children were made in the staffroom than was the case at Towne, nor was there unreadiness to take them. The head believed that there was a case for keeping the Lower Remove children as far as possible with one teacher, and not exposing them to a full specialist programme, which she felt they were less ready for than the abler children. At the same time, they enjoyed their visits to the gym, the art-room, and the housecraft room. Their class teacher, who had them for general subjects for about half of their timetable, was a somewhat unexciting but stable woman. She was less scholastically able than Mrs Hall, but her accepting attitudes and her genuine concern for the welfare of her girls made her a valuable member of staff, and her head was quick to recognize and appreciate her services. Instead of trying to turn her into something she wasn't, the head used her where she could be most helpful. Equally, instead of trying to turn these girls into something they weren't or bemoaning that it was impossible while making no effort to find a substitute positive goal, the staff as a whole were ready to accept them for what they were and to work from there. So there was a much more positive feeling about all the work that was done with the less able children throughout the school.

In many respects – size, district, buildings, streamed organization – these two schools were comparable, yet there was a marked difference in their tone, particularly as it was reflected in the less able children. The success of Othertown in solving what is often regarded as an insoluble problem, how to prevent the less able children from sticking out like a sore thumb, should warn us against adopting a defeatist point of view as being inevitable. It is certainly true that slow learners present more difficulties to their teachers for very obvious reasons – they are harder to motivate, the carrot of examination success cannot be applied, failure is a constantly inhibiting factor, it is more difficult for them to realize the value of work that may to them appear unrealistic and meaningless – and to that extent they are more at risk as far as school adjustment is concerned.

Rather than rehearsing, as is so often done, the all too familiar tale of concomitants of backwardness – emotional instability, poor homes, deprived neighbourhoods, personal inadequacy, social immaturity, and the rest – it seems to me much more valuable to rephrase the question in a more positive fashion and ask 'Under what circumstances can these depressing vicious circles be avoided?' 'How can the morale of the slower children be built up, instead of being further lowered, in school?' So while readily agreeing that slow learners are more at risk, I would deny that they must inevitably become discipline problems just as one can hold *both* that children in a deprived slum area are more at risk for delinquency *and* that nevertheless the majority of these children yet do not become delinquent. The relationship here is not a logical one of entailment, and we do not help matters by confusing what *may* (under unfavourable circumstances) happen with what *must* happen. At the present time too many teachers are bemused by (valid) research figures of the relationship between backwardness at school and various forms of criminality and personal maladjustment, and reach the (invalid) conclusion that these must inescapably follow, and hence fall into a form of defeatism which is most likely to bring about the consequences that are feared.

Certainly all my experience has repeatedly emphasized that teachers who believe in the children they are teaching may gain results against all the odds, while those who despise and reject children on whatever grounds are more likely to have a disciplinary problem on their hands, however excellent the home background, and however clever the children.

What, then, can we learn from the contrasted examples of these two otherwise similar schools that will help us in finding positive applications, not just reasons why things should (and by an easy transition in our thoughts, must) go wrong? The clear difference is in the attitudes and values of the staffs, presumably deriving at least to some extent from the heads. The head of Towne had many virtues – she was energetic, hardworking, purposeful, and humane. But when it came to the point her humanity took second place to her wish to run a 'successful' school, where 'success' was defined in narrow terms of obvious and easily measurable goals. The priorities she set herself are illuminating – the timetable filled up first for the examination forms and the removes put in at the end, the encouragement to girls to stay on to do advanced work so that much of the art teacher's time, for example, is taken up with two girls, the readiness to transfer Mrs Hall to solve an immediately apparent problem without looking at the underlying causative factors. These actions show her implicit values, which are all of a piece. It is true that Mrs Hall is given a good allowance and a free hand – but only because of the need to contain a pressing problem. Would it not, however, have been wiser to look more deeply at the *causes* of the disaffection with a view to preventing its occurring in future? In such an atmosphere, the staff develop their own discriminations. They may grumble among themselves at the disproportionate size of teaching groups at the top of the school with the large classes of younger and less able children, but since kudos comes from the former rather than the latter it is obviously to their advantage to press as hard as they can for their own share of examination work. Their own values are shaped in the process. The vicious circle then begins by which they see less credit likely to come to them from their work with slow learners, which in any case is less immediately rewarding in terms of reassurance of their teaching skill and the more gratifying forms of feedback. Mrs Hall to some extent cuts across this value system. She influences the housecraft teacher in an opposite direction, and she is strengthened by her own seniority, though obviously her influence is much less pervasive than that of the ruling hierarchy of the school. In Othertown, it is the head who by her all-round fairness sees to it that all children have a fair crack of the whip and so the hardened attitudes of Towne do not get a chance to form. Children are taken much more at face value there and the narrow constrictiveness leading to vicious circles of negative attitude, negative response, and an all-round atmosphere of blame and resistance do not develop.

★   ★   ★

This example showed the key role of the head as a determinant of morale, and though most attention was given to the attitudes and reactions of the children, something was said of the staff's part in the value system. In the next study, the focus is on the relationship between head and staff, with little mention of the children. The duration here is over a period of five years.

3 Staff Morale

At a time when amalgamations are frequent, it may be worth while to examine by means of a case study some of the factors involved in the waxing and waning of staff morale. The example is not intended as a criticism of comprehensive reorganization, but it *is* a plea for deliberate consideration of issues of morale, for, without good morale among the staff, even the most enlightened schemes can fail to reach their full effectiveness.

Three secondary modern schools were joined to form the basis of a new comprehensive school. The district was a reasonably good one, and all three schools had a good reputation and none had any difficulty in attracting and keeping staff. One was much larger than the other two, so that it tended to dominate in inter-school sporting and other fixtures. Rivalry among the children did not degenerate into bitterness. Relationships between the various staffs though friendly were not close, and one of the smaller schools thought itself more advanced in its ideas than the others which were more traditional.

As there was no grammar school among the original components, the development of a new academic element was thought to be of great importance, and much weight was naturally put on this in the selection of the headmaster. Mr Smith came from outside the area with experience that had been exclusively in grammar schools. He was friendly, pleasant, and approachable, and his appointment was very well received by his prospective colleagues. It was recognized that his bias was not theirs but it was accepted that emphasis on the new grammar side was inevitable, and, since he made a good first impression as a person, everything seemed set fair. The school moved into its new premises, additional graduate staff were appointed, and everyone began the process of shaking down together.

This case history will trace how, in spite of the many favourable factors involved, goodwill was gradually dissipated and staff morale suffered. To begin with, all was honey. Most people were on their best behaviour, and were almost too effusively cooperative. The tensions that had been inherited from the past among the staff were kept in the background. A joint revision of syllabuses was put into effect at once and frequent staff meetings considered them. There was a feeling of eagerness at being in on the start of something big and important, with an expectation of higher status to accrue for the school from the much greater emphasis now to be given to examination work, particularly in the development of a much bigger sixth form. Not everyone liked the new buildings – in spite of their spaciousness, they didn't seem homely – but most people were proud of their bright new image.

Doubts came slowly. Unfortunately Mr Smith was not a very good administrator, and staff meetings tended to drag on rather aimlessly with no very clear agenda and a general feeling that it was democratic to have meetings irrespective of what went on at them. Irrelevances were unchecked, and multiplied: much time was taken in the discussion of trivial issues like the design of the new school crest and it was only gradually realized that important decisions on matters of principle had been taken without any fig-leaf of staff consultation. A certain scepticism that the democratic approach was only a façade crept in: however justified or unjustified this scepticism may have been, it was itself destructive. Some saw that Mr Smith had a thankless task, and felt more irritated with their colleagues for their red herrings than with Mr Smith for his failure to check them, hanging on as long as possible to the 'superman' adulation with which they had first surrounded him. But gradually it became evident that, irrelevant as many of the speakers may have been, the worse difficulty lay in Mr Smith's over-casual attitude. He didn't really regard the meetings as serious or important enough to prepare for. What *did* he regard seriously? Only his academic programme.

This was the danger point, at which the 'old' staff began to feel themselves devalued. It was not merely that they had to make room for new commitments, new objectives, alongside their own. This they were expecting, and were ready to welcome at least consciously – no doubt there were also unconscious or semi-conscious ambivalences and reservations all along. But what they were not expecting was the total incomprehension they received and the lack of recognition of their efforts.

'He isn't interested.' 'He doesn't know.' 'Well, at least he leaves us alone.' 'We need more leadership.' 'He should take more part in the school as a whole.' 'He's entirely absorbed in the grammar side.' 'I wish he'd come round and see what we were doing.' 'He wouldn't know what to look for if he did.' These comments are the comments of lowering morale. The use of the word 'side' is particularly significant. Sides *were* being taken and the staff were splitting on them. So the cracks appeared, and the lines of cleavage became evident.

In a situation where the majority of the staff feel themselves threatened and undervalued, several things tend to happen. First, they became over-insistent on their contribution, as if they felt they had to call attention to it because otherwise it would get overlooked. Some of the irrelevances may have been due to this insecurity, and meetings tended increasingly to be interrupted by personal glorifications. Secondly, the formation of sides was intensified. Thirdly, in a deteriorating climate suspicions run riot. In an atmosphere of goodwill, mistakes can be made and rectified without too much loss of face, but when trust is gone, suspicions multiply beyond the bounds of reason. Fourthly, an over-tense, over-touchy climate is engendered. Worst of all, is the distraction that all this brings from what should be the main purpose of a school staff, the welfare and progress of the pupils – *all* the pupils, not just the ones that were thought likely to bring kudos on the school by reason of their abilities, intellectual or sporting.

So after two years much of the initial goodwill had evaporated and underlying tensions were appearing on the surface. Here are some particular examples of incidents thereafter that show the deteriorating position.

1. Mr Smith, in an unguarded moment, spoke to the head of the English department of the latter's work as 'sterile'. 'There's nothing to show for it', he said. This man had insisted on retaining himself a fair amount of non-examination work, rather than teaching only examination forms, as he could easily have done. He was both infuriated and dismayed – and also hurt. He realized that it was a slip on Mr Smith's part, but a significant slip since it showed his true attitude and values. As he was himself one of Mr Smith's recent appointees, his deteriorating morale was all the more noticeable.

2. The County sent round a memorandum containing altered arrangements for graded posts. The heads of departments all disliked it and said so. Mr Smith amiably agreed to take up the matter without really bothering to find out the issues involved. His letter to the County sat neatly on the fence, managing to suggest that his colleagues could have taken up the matter themselves much earlier if only they had troubled, and supporting them so lukewarmly that it was worse than nothing. It was pointed out to him at a heated meeting by his irate colleagues that in fact they had *not* been dilatory, and he apologized for this mis-statement. Although mollified by his frankness, his colleagues were not inclined to let the matter drop and they appointed a small delegation to go with Mr Smith to approach the County. Evidently they did not trust Mr Smith on his own. Mr Smith, who had never taken the matter really seriously, for the first time understood the depth of feeling on the issue and agreed to this suggestion. Feelings at this stage were best expressed by one of the delegates who said, 'He could have told us right at the beginning he wouldn't support us. If he'd said – The County has spoken, pipe down – we wouldn't have

liked it but we would have respected him and we probably would have taken seriously any advice from him that our case wasn't good enough. Or else he should have supported us properly. As it is, I don't think he ever took the trouble to find out what our case was.' After this débâcle, Mr Smith wrote a second time to the County setting out his colleagues' misgivings fully and carefully. He circulated this letter, and they were satisfied.

Time dragged on and still the delegation had not been received. Reminders to Mr Smith were impatiently received – a lot of fuss about nothing – and doubts began to revive. Eventually the delegation was received, months later, and an acceptable compromise reached. But the final blow to morale came by chance. At this meeting, Mr Smith's second letter to the County was accidentally handed to a delegate. It had a scribbled addition next to the signature, 'Sorry about this nonsense'. By trying to keep in with everybody, and by failing to act at any point on principle, Mr Smith had forfeited his claim to respect.

3. A year or so later, reorganization was in the air. A group of senior masters had been asked to examine and report on the merits of different schemes of organization. They did this very thoroughly and eventually came out with a recommendation that the school should go over to a house-based organization; whereas previously it had been year-based. Obviously no solution would please everybody, but they felt that the balance of advantage lay with the scheme they recommended, and this was their reply over and over again as points of detail were brought up in discussion. The deputy head, who was in the chair because Mr Smith was absent ill, eventually said there had been enough discussion and asked for a motion, clearly expecting it to pass without difficulty. But the motion came from one of the younger masters, and asked for the report to be referred back to the subcommittee for further consideration of points raised. In a close vote, this motion was carried. The subcommittee were naturally dismayed at this lack of appreciation of their efforts, and pointed out with annoyance that they had already considered those issues and nothing new was likely to

emerge, only a waste of time. The deputy head stood firm, and said that, since the matter had come to a vote, the decision should stand. With a bad grace the seniors finally accepted this.

This episode does not concern Mr Smith, but it is instructive in several respects. On the face of it, it was a fairly irrational decision, since nothing was likely to be achieved except delay, muddle, and uncertainty – so what prompted it? It can best be regarded, I suggest, as a symptom of low morale and frustration, directed on this occasion, not against Mr Smith, but against the oligarchy of powerful figures. Just as the headmaster was a target for ambivalence in the previous incidents described, so in their turn the oligarchy were liable to arouse similar feelings of distrust and non-cooperation, irrespective of the objective value and rationality of their proposals. What mattered to the 'common man' was that this was his one opportunity to show his independence. As one said afterwards, 'I didn't know much about it either way, but as there were so many doubts expressed, I thought it had better go back.'

The final point is, is it entirely a coincidence that, in a situation where there is absence of trust between the head and 'middle management', there is also likely to be a lack of trust between the oligarchy and the rank and file? Lack of trust is infectious, and so is bloody-mindedness.

4. When the deputy head retired, there was a prolonged interregnum before a new appointment was made. During this time, rumours were rife, cabals were formed, plots suspected at every turn. Eventually, things settled down, but there was no longer any pretence, as there had been in the first years of the new school, that everything in the garden was lovely.

In the light of these examples, how did things go wrong? Inefficiency, poor organization, lack of preparation before meetings, were the first signs but in themselves would probably not have carried much weight against the generally good 'image' of Mr Smith and of the new school. It is interesting how much carelessness and inefficiency can be tolerated in a situation where there is general goodwill: it is when the goodwill comes to be questioned that the more serious blows to morale come. Thus, for instance, in another school the head had been quite as slack as Mr Smith and a deadline had been missed. The master immediately responsible explained to his colleagues and apologized: Mr Brown (the head) intervened to say it was not the master's fault and that if anyone was to blame it was himself. All this was taken very calmly by everyone and public sympathy was decidedly on the side of the master, who it was realized would be put to considerable inconvenience to overcome the effects of the mistake, and of the head, who oddly seemed more human for having slipped up. It seems very unfair that Mr Brown's position *vis-à-vis* his colleagues should have been if anything strengthened by carelessness as great as Mr Smith's. The difference, surely, is that Mr Brown was guilty of carelessness alone, which can be condoned, but carelessness that has its root in indifference to the values and feelings of one's colleagues cannot be. A popular boy can get away with conduct that would call down howls of execration on an unpopular one, and similarly in a situation of good morale errors can be tolerated that would be heavily complained about if the morale was poor. It seems that what really matters is the basic feeling of trust or confidence, and that when this is disturbed everything fails. Presumably if Mr Brown *continued* to make errors, a point would come when his staff began to say, 'The old man isn't what he used to be', and doubt would creep in whether on *this* new occasion he was going to be adequate. It is as if he had over the years accrued a favourable balance sheet that could be drawn upon in case of need to erase the occasional debit entry. Credit is a matter of confidence, as long as there is not a run on the bank, which is itself more likely to be provoked when confidence is impaired. So once Mr Smith had lost the confidence of his staff, he had lost his greatest asset.

I conclude that the head of a school may, in the first instance, be endowed *ex officio* with almost 'magical' powers by his subordinates who wish to see him as superman. As long as this confidence persists, all is well, but if for any reason this seeps away, the

other side of the balance comes into play and he becomes the
target of suspicion, as formerly of adulation; of mistrust, as
formerly of security. Group morale will either sustain him or, by
its absence, weaken him.

★   ★   ★

In contrast to the deteriorating situation described above, let us
turn now to a more hopeful case, where the change is in a positive
direction, and where the appointment of a new head produced a
marked improvement in the attitudes of both staff and children –
but not miraculously, not quickly, and not without a lot of hard
work.

4 On the Up-grade

Mr Walker had been headmaster of Gaymount Primary School for a number of years. He had the reputation of being 'rather an old misery' very ready to see the worst side of everything. Visitors from the local Education Office were usually received with grumbles, often on matters which they felt to be trivial, so they tended to keep away: he then felt neglected, and the occasional genuinely important matter was left undealt with longer than it need have been, to give him further cause for complaint He had been disappointed not to get another school, and the transfer of Gaymount into a new building about three years before he retired did not mollify him. Instead he grumbled at the work involved and spent much time complaining of minor (but real) faults in fitments. The whole building *did* look drab in spite of its newness and in spite of its name, but this may have been due to the roughness and carelessness of the children, and the apathy of the staff. The school was situated in a decayed inner area of a large northern city: it was a difficult district and Mr Walker was quite right in saying that it had gone down a good deal, so that recent admissons tended to be more uncouth than formerly. Discipline was not good, and this naturally led to unhappiness and frequent changes among the staff. Mid-morning and lunch breaks tended to stretch out longer than they should have done, and when finally the bell rang and the children returned to their classrooms, there was little to hold their interest. The curriculum was pedestrian. One of the few things Mr Walker was concerned about was swimming, and everything was subordinated to this, until in the end the tail wagged the dog and even the music specialist spent more time escorting children to and from the baths than she did at her main task. Here then, is a school where staff morale was low, and where the new head would have a difficult assignment. To make matters worse, there was a term's gap between the departure of Mr Walker and the arrival of Mr Day, during which time the deputy was in charge. The deputy, who had been a candidate for the headship and very disappointed not to get it, asked for a transfer and left when Mr Day arrived. This was Mr Day's first headship: he was keen and enthusiastic and naturally anxious to succeed, but he found himself in a daunting situation where his very keenness could easily have led him into injudicious action and where good intentions were no guarantee of success.

1st Term. Almost his first job was to find a deputy. His staff of eleven consisted of six who were in their first or second year of teaching, including one mature woman; two temporaries, of whom one was an Indian with a law degree but no teacher training; and three who had been at the school for some years. One of these had poor health, another was frequently absent without the excuse of bad health, and only one seemed remotely possible as a deputy. He was very tempted to bring fresh blood in from outside, but finally, with the advice of his local inspector, settled on the internal candidate. The new deputy had a good record of loyal unspectacular service: the appointment was thus an indication that this would be valued and not passed over in a search for more glittering qualifications. It did much to get the staff on his side. He was also aided by their natural willingness to change from the previous dreary regime (though it should be hastily added that this willingness to change did not at first include their own easy-going habits). He found the standards very low, but irked as he was by them decided to bide his time. His first priority was to improve the general order of the school, and in this he was willingly backed by the staff, because it was obviously in their interests that the children's behaviour in and around the school should be improved. Secondly, he took the opportunity to do as much teaching as he could himself. As there were some notorious absentees on the staff, he had plenty of opportunity. The teachers on their side were glad that he did not push double classes on to them, but was willing to work alongside them, and their initial cautious welcome of him became warmer. He genuinely enjoyed teaching, and valued it in others, and he was prepared to support the youngsters and encourage the inexperienced older woman. In all this, his administrative duties took second place. His part-time secretary was given more responsibility, and responded well. The things that *had* to be done by him he did after school hours, and he was very rarely in his room. He preferred to be seen at breaks and in the dinner hour round the corridors, and the school discipline correspondingly improved. After the first few weeks, he felt secure enough of the goodwill of the teachers to tighten the punctuality of bells after break, and a generally more purposeful, cohesive spirit began to be felt among both staff and children. He was approachable and friendly, but firm. He took care not to moan about non-essentials and to keep the matters on which he was dissatisfied but had no means of improving as yet to himself: thus he presented always a positive and encouraging front to the teachers. The cook and the caretaker soon became his allies.

By the end of the term the children seemed more settled, and the teachers were correspondingly happier in their ability to control them. It was becoming more evident which of the teachers (the majority) were prepared to pull their weight, and which couldn't, or wouldn't be bothered, to help to improve standards of work.

2nd Term. Two new appointments were made to replace the two temporaries who had left, and these strengthened the staff. The swimming timetable, which could not be touched in the previous term because of the need to give a term's notice at the baths, was now cut down somewhat and made more coherent and less time-wasting. Other tentative developments occurred – music here, drama there, an educational visit or two – signs that the teachers were, with improved morale, showing greater confidence and interest in their work. So the vicious circle of apathy in the staff and bad behaviour and destructiveness among the children was gradually overcome. Parents noticed the change. They were more welcome when they called, even to complain, and there was a red-letter day when the first father appeared, not to complain, but to offer help. A visiting inspector commented, 'Even the building looks brighter as I approach it.' He knew that this was not so, and that he was merely projecting his own more hopeful feelings on to the exterior, but it was significant. Inside, the building was certainly brighter and better kept.

Mr Day now began to feel that he could make greater demands on the staff without endangering the good relations that he had been at such pains to build. To begin with he had accepted any suggestions for outside visits to widen the children's experience, but he now began to ensure that the visits were used for a genuinely educational purpose before sanctioning them, and that they were being properly prepared and followed up. The staff got the message, that whatever they did had to be purposeful and that it was not enough just to 'prettify' the curriculum. The tone of staffroom conversation changed, with less gossip and more genuine interest in the rationale of teaching. It is not surprising that standards in the basic subjects improved and that lessons were better planned. Mr Day was also able to give more direct long-term guidance – as distinct from first-aid – to those who wanted help.

3rd Term. Things continued to improve. The old reputation of being a dead-end school had gone. The deputy began to blossom. Several of the younger members of staff took a lively part in district affairs. A warm and welcoming atmosphere was evident to visitors to the staffroom. During the (necessary) absence of one of the teachers, groups of the oldest children were allowed to get on on their own and on each occasion behaved so sensibly that they drew commendation from Mr Day. At another time when two of his teachers left early to attend a meeting he commented to his secretary that he would take both classes himself rather than put additional burdens on anyone else. It was this willingness to join in himself, and not stand aloof in fancied dignity, which was responsible as much as anything in gaining Mr Day the respect and cooperation of his staff, and the great improvement in their morale.

When we look at this success story (not by any means easily won), what factors can be perceived in it?

1. Mr Day was no doubt fortunate in having a friendly and attractive manner, to which adults and children quickly responded. But personal charm and friendliness are not enough. Unless they are also added to genuine concern for those working with him, and a readiness to consider their interests as well as his own, they will soon be shown to be hollow, as we saw with Mr Smith in the previous study.

2. There was an absence of defensiveness and a readiness to go in as man to man. It is true that he had not much to lose, and everything to gain if the school could be pulled up, yet perhaps this makes the absence of defensiveness all the more striking. What we get above all from him is the flavour of enjoyment. Difficult as the school was, he was enjoying tackling his problems. 'I think it's going to be one of those days,' he remarked with great composure and a cheerful smile when faced with an accident report, a visitor, a gang of workmen, and two staff absent – all this on the day of a medical inspection.

3. The importance of timing. He did not try to do too much too quickly, and so fail to carry his teachers with him. Instead, he settled his priorities and stuck to them, and left other matters (however important) to a later occasion. In this he was sharply contrasted to his predecessor, who tended to waste his energies on non-essentials, and who didn't get very far for a large expenditure of effort, partly because he antagonized those in a position to help him, and failed to give a clear lead to those whom he could have helped – his young teachers.

4. Again in contrast to Mr Walker, Mr Day was always positive. He was always ready to praise and give appreciation where it was deserved (e.g. in the appointment of a deputy, and in the behaviour of the eleven-year-olds when left to get on by themselves). So morale grew, by building up a feeling that effort was worth while. Even the cleaners shared in this, and took an interest in the purposes of the school.

5. Mr Day was not gimmicky. He was not concerned just to put on an attractive show, but wanted to be convinced that what was done was of genuine use, e.g. his action over the visits, and his encouragement of improving standards in basic subjects as well as the more immediately attractive ones such as drama and art. So he could gain respect as well as liking.

6. At the same time, he was ready to wait and did not try to drive his teachers – a deadly temptation to an ambitious newly appointed head. Although he worked hard himself and encouraged his teachers to do the same, he was not exacting nor did he try to force the pace. He did not, for example, arrange an endless series of staff meetings after school like Mr Smith in the previous study, or try to push everyone on evening courses, or make demands that were felt to be too heavy. When staff meetings were held they were brief, necessary, and well run, with plenty of notice given beforehand. He geared his expectations to what people were able to give, and was ready to temper the wind to the shorn lamb. Since his teachers had their individual strengths and weaknesses he did not expect the same dead level of performance, much less of perfection, from all, but was prepared to meet them at the point where they were and start encouraging them from there. By this means he retained the positive attitude mentioned earlier, and encouraged rather than drove, his staff forward.

7. It is tempting to ask, how much was this done of deliberate purpose, by cool calculation of the policies most likely to improve morale? and how much was intuitive, a natural response of a friendly outgoing personality to a complicated and constantly changing interplay of circumstances which could not possibly

worked out in set terms beforehand? This question would be very difficult to answer. Probably both applied, for while common sense and forethought might dictate the outlines of a policy, unless it was broadly in line with his basic attitudes – friendliness, respect for others – it could hardly have been carried out consistently over a long period of time and under constant pressure. It is an important question to ask, nevertheless, for it raises the issue how far skill in morale-raising is communicable and can be consciously gained by striving.

8. A final question – how far was Mr Walker's pessimism infectious, so that many of the difficulties he faced radiated from him, while on the other hand Mr Day's enjoyment also communicated itself to others? Presumably (to link this with the last) Mr Walker also was capable of rationally calculating the chances of alternative lines of action and of seeing the advantages of policies which he did *not* put into practice. Or was he? Which is the chicken, and which the egg?

*   *   *

One of the points that was raised above concerned Mr Day's absence of drive and hurry; rather than rush into a gimmicky solution, he was ready to wait and allow genuine growth to take place. What happens, however, when outside pressures are put on schools to achieve results quickly?

5 *The Office wants Results Quickly*

An administrator wanted information about a candidate for a headship, and telephoned his opposite number in the Authority from which the candidate came. He explained that the school had rather run down and he wanted to get it put 'on the map' (1). He wanted it to be better than any other similar school (2). Would Mr X be capable of impressing himself, not only in his own school, but in relation to all the other schools of the district? (3). Was Mr X well up in the very latest methods? (4). Did he believe in the integrated day? (5). When the respondent tried to stress Mr X's solid worth, he seemed uninterested. He asked no questions about Mr X's organizational capacity.

Comments

1. Does the use of this phrase imply that he would be unduly impressed by quick results and gimmicky publicity?
2. How realistic is this desire? especially when, as he says, it is at present in rather bad shape.
3. Again the suggestion that a publicist is what is wanted – one who will make an immediate impact irrespective of its soundness.
4. As between two candidates with similar qualifications one of whom had gained them ten years previously (and therefore had time to put his knowledge into effect) and the other one year

previously, he seemed to assume that the former by that very fact must be out of date.

5. In a type of school where the integrated day was not especially relevant.

This short example is included to show that pressures from outside can affect the desirable rate of change in a school. Let us suppose that Mr Day, of the previous example, had been appointed head of this school. What chance would he have had to go at his own pace, and consolidate his gains, if he had had a militantly 'progressive' District Education Officer breathing down his neck? Just as children sometimes work more productively and less anxiously when not driven by teachers, just as teachers sometimes work more productively and less anxiously when not driven by heads, so heads in their turn may benefit from being allowed to take their time. So often the examples are all the other way – the children driven by the teachers, the teachers kept up to scratch by the heads, the heads striving to fulfil the demands of 'the office' – or at least *feeling themselves* to be so driven. The result of this anxious following of fashion is to be seen in many places and is surely an example of low teacher-morale, since so much of their efforts are not inner-directed, from what they *know* to be valuable, but other-directed, from a feverish wish to keep up with the pace-setters, the educational Joneses.

★   ★   ★

So far the examples chosen have been mainly on the negative side – the positive has come indirectly as a sort of contrast to the negative pole which has been more fully described. Even Mr Day has been introduced in a context that leaves much to be desired.

It is in fact very much easier to portray an unsatisfactory situation than to portray a satisfactory one in depth. Why should this be so? Mainly because the satisfactory one so often seems rather colourless, quiet, easy. Nothing is happening – apparently. Things are achieved easily and without effort – apparently. Everyone concerned behaves so well that it looks as if there is nothing in it – apparently. Just as the law-abiding citizen does not achieve the notoriety in the local paper of his delinquent brother, just as educational books with lurid titles (*Blackboard Jungle*, etc.) and exciting revelations of dreadful goings-on in slum schools are more immediately interesting (because sensational) than more sober volumes, so an attempt to describe in detail a well-ordered class-room, school, or community seems pi, or far-fetched, or just plain dull. When we use the methods of the time-samplers as Anderson and his associates (1946) did in their studies of teachers' classroom personalities and the relations of these to the social climate of the classroom, even in this microscopic situation it is still easier to see the causal links of mistaken handling than of good handling. Gardner and Cass (1965) were attempting something very valuable and very difficult in quantifying the *positive* interactions between teacher and pupil, as was Webb (1967) in her study of ways in which children with quite severe problems of adjustment had been helped by teachers within the ordinary infant school framework and without any special mystique. When things go well, it isn't news – but the smooth-running class or lecture-room are just as much examples of causal chains as are the disturbed ones. Certainly we can, as Batten (1967) has said, if we are humble enough, learn from what has gone wrong before and resolve to avoid those errors in future, but it is even more important, and more rarely done, to consider why things went right. So the common focusing of case studies on errors, though natural, does not seem to be enough, and should be supplemented by a focus on the positive and the excellent, so that we may if possible learn in what this excellence consists. Examples of good procedure are to be found in the study by Gardner and Cass already mentioned, and in books such as *Village School* ('Miss Read', 1955), and *An Experiment in Education* (Marshall, 1963), which give straightforward accounts of the ongoing progress of a school over a period of time, showing the web of interactions between children and teachers. So my next example will come from *Village School* – a long transcript followed by comments. Although in one sense it has been fic-tionalized, it could not have been written without long experience and in a more important sense is undeniably authentic.

6 Village School

(It is the first day back after the summer holidays. Miss Read describes the settling in. The transcript is taken from the sections entitled 'The Pattern of the Morning' and 'The Pattern of the Afternoon'.)

The Pattern of the Morning

My desk was being besieged by children, all eager to tell me of their holiday adventures.

'Miss, us went to Southsea with the Mothers' Union last week, and I've brought you back a stick of rock,' announced Anne.

Eric flapped a long rubbery piece of seaweed like a flail. 'It's for us to tell the weather by,' he explained earnestly. 'You hangs it up – out the lobby'll do – and if it's wet it's going to rain – or is it if it's been wet it feels wet? I forgets just which, miss, but anyhow if it's dry it ain't going to rain.,

'Isn't,' I corrected automatically, rummaging in the top drawer of the desk for the dinner book.

'I know where there's mushrooms, miss. I'll bring you some for your tea s'afternoon.'

'They're not mushrooms, miss,' warned Eric. 'They's toad-stools – honest, miss! Don't you eat 'em, miss! They's poison!'

I waved them away to their desks. Only the new children

stood self-consciously in the front, looking at their shoes or at me for support. Linda Moffat's immaculate pink frock and glossy curls were getting a close scrutiny from the other children, but, unperturbed, she returned their round-eyed stares.

The children sit two in a desk and Anne, a cheerful nine-year-old, seemed Linda's best desk-mate.

'Look after Linda, Anne,' I said, 'she doesn't know anyone yet.'

Holding her diminutive red handbag, Linda settled down beside Anne. They gave each other covert looks under their lashes, and when their glances met exchanged smiles.

The four young ones, just up from Miss Clare's class, settled in two desks at the front. Once sitting in safety their shyness vanished, and they looked cheerfully about, grinning at their friends. They were at that engaging stage of losing their front milk teeth, and their gappy smiles emphasized their tender years. I went over to the piano.

'As we haven't given out the hymn-books yet, we'll sing one we know by heart.'

They scrambled to their feet, desk seats clanging up behind them, and piped 'The King of Love my Shepherd is', rather sharp with excitement. . . .

Usually the whole school comes into this one classroom for prayers, but on the first morning of term it always seems best to stay in our own rooms and settle in quickly.

After the hymn we had a short prayer. With eyes screwed up tightly and hands solemnly folded beneath their chins the children looked misleadingly angelic. Patrick, the smallest, with head bowed low, was busily sucking his thumb, and I made a mental note that here was a habit to be corrected or otherwise his new second teeth would soon be in need of a brace. As I watched, a shilling fell from his clasped hands and rolled noisily towards me. Patrick opened one eye. It swivelled round like a solitaire marble, following the shilling's journey, then, catching my own eye upon it, it shut again with a snap.

After prayers we usually have a scripture lesson, or learn a new hymn or a psalm, until half-past nine, when arithmetic lesson begins; but on this morning we settled to more practical matters and the children came out in turn with their dinner money for the week. This was ninepence a day. Some children had also brought National Savings money, and this was entered in a separate book and stamps handed over to the child, if it possessed a safe place to put them, or put in a special Oxo tin until home time.

All but four children, who went home for their dinners, brought out their dinner money, and as they put it on my desk I looked at their hands. Sometimes they arrive at school so filthy, either through playing with mud on the way, or through sheer neglect in washing, that they are not fit to handle their books, and then out they are sent to the stone sink in the lobby, to wash in rainwater and carbolic soap. In this way too I can keep a watch on the nail-biters, and those culprits who, after a week's self-control, can show a proud sixteenth of an inch, are rewarded with sweets and flattery. Scabies, too, which first shows itself between the fingers, is a thing to watch for, though, happily, it is rare here; but it spreads quickly and is very aggravating to the sufferer.

While I was busy with all this, Miss Clare came through the partition door.

'May I speak to Cathy?' she asked. 'It's about Joseph's dinner money. Does his mother want him to stay?'

'Yes, miss,' said Cathy, looking rathei startled, 'but she never gave me no money for him.'

'Didn't give me any money,' said Miss Clare automatically.

'"Didn't-give-me-any-money", I mean,' repeated Cathy, parrot-wise.

'I'll write a note for you to take to Mrs Coggs when you go home,' said Miss Clare, and lowering her voice to a discreet whisper, turned to me.

'May be difficult to get the money regularly from that family – a feckless woman!' And shaking her white head she returned to the infants.

The children were now beginning to get restless, for, normally, when I was busy they would take out a library book, or a note-book of their own making, which we called a 'busy book', in which they could employ themselves in writing lists of birds, flowers, makes of cars, or any other things which interested them. They could, if they liked, copy down the multiplication tables, or the weekly poem or spelling list which hung upon the wall; but, at the moment, their desks were empty.

'Let me see who would like to come out and play "Left and Right",' I said.

Peace reigned at once. Chests were flung out and faces assumed a fierce air of responsibility and trustworthiness.

'Patrick!' I called, choosing the smallest new boy, and he flushed a deep pink with pleasure.

'Left and Right' is the simplest and most absorbing game for occasions when a teacher is busy with something else. All that is needed is a small object to hide in one hand, a morsel of chalk, a bead or a halfpenny, any one, in fact, of the small things that litter the inkstand. The child in front, hands behind him, changes the treasure from one to the other; then, fists extended before him, he challenges someone to guess which hand it is in. Here the teacher, with half an eye on the game, one and a half on the business in hand, and her main object peace in which to carry it out, can say, 'Choose someone really quiet, dear. No fussy people; and, of course, no one who asks!' This deals a severe blow to the naughty little boys who are whispering 'Me! Choose me! Or else —!'

'Richard!' called Patrick to his desk-mate.

'Left!'

'No, right!' said Patrick, opening a sticky palm.

'That's left! Miss, that was left!' went up the protesting cry. Patrick turned round to me indignantly.

'But you're facing the other way now!' I point out, and the age-long problem, which puzzles all children, had to be explained yet again.

At last the game continued its even tenor. Dinner money and

savings money were both collected, checked and put in their separate tins. The register was called for the first time, and a neat red stroke in every square showed that we were all present.

The clock on the wall said twenty-past ten when we had finished handing out a pink exercise book each for English, a blue for arithmetic and a green for history and geography. Readers, pens, pencils, rulers and all the other paraphernalia of daily school life were now stored safely, and at the moment tidily, in their owner's possession.

The children collected milk and straws and settled down to refreshment. Luckily this term there were no milk-haters and all twenty-two bottles were soon emptied. When they had finished they went joyfully out to play.

I went across to my own quiet house and switched on the kettle. Two cups and saucers were already set on the tray in the kitchen, and the biscuits tin stood on the dresser. Miss Clare would be over in a minute. We took it in turns to do playground duty, guarding the coke pile from marauders, watching out for any sly teasing, and routing out the indoor-lovers who would prefer to sit in their desks even on the loveliest day. I went back to the playground while the kettle boiled.

Linda was undoing her packet of chocolate and Anne was trying to look unconcerned. Anne was always rather hungry, the child of a mother who went by early morning bus to the atomic research works some miles away, and who had little time to leave such niceties as elevenses for her daughter. There was no shortage of money in this home, but definitely a shortage of supervision. Anne's shoes were good, but dirty; her dinner money was often forgotten, and her socks frequently sported a hole. Her suspense now was short-lived, for Linda broke off a generous piece of her slab, handed it over, and cemented the friendship which had already begun.

'D'you mind being new?' asked Anne squelchily.

'Not now,' answered Linda, 'once all that staring's stopped, I don't mind; and if anyone tries hitting me my mum said I was to tell her.' She eyes the noisy children around her complacently.

'Not that they will, probably – and anyway,' she added, dropping her voice to a sinister whisper, 'I bites horrible!' Anne looked properly impressed.

Cathy, between bites of apple, was encouraging Joseph Coggs and her young brother to visit the boys' lavatory behind its green corrugated iron screen. At the other end of the playground, similarly screened, were two more bucket-type lavatories with well-scrubbed wooden seats, for the girls' use.

Mr Willet is our caretaker, and has the unenviable job of emptying the buckets three times a week; and this he does into deep holes which are dug on a piece of waste ground, some hundred yards away, behind his own cottage.

Mrs Pringle, the school cleaner, scrubs seats and floors, and everything is kept as spotless as is possible with this deplorable and primitive type of sanitation.

Above the shouting of the children came the sound of the school gate clanging shut, and across the playground, his black suit glossy in the sunlight, came the vicar. Miss Clare hurried in to fetch another cup and saucer from the dresser and I went to meet him.

The Reverend Gerald Partridge has been vicar of Fairacre, and its adjoining parish of Beech Green, for only four years, and so is looked upon as a foreigner by most of his parishioners. His energetic wife is as brisk and practical as he is gentle and vague. He is chairman of the managers of Fairacre school and comes in every Friday morning to take a scripture lesson with the older children.

On this morning, he carried a list of hymns, which he asked me to teach the children during the term, and I said I would look through them. He sighed at my guarded answer, for he knew as well as I did that not all the hymns would be considered suitable by me for teaching to children. His weakness for the metaphysical poets led him into choosing quite inexplicable hymns about showers and brides, with lines like:

'Rend each man's temple-veil and bid it fall,'

or, worse still, Milton's poems set as hymns, containing such lines as:

> 'And speckled vanity
> Will sicken soon and die,
> And leprous sin will melt from earthy mould,'

all of which may be fine in its way but is quite beyond the comprehension of the pupils here. The vicar smiles and nods his mild old head when I protest.

'Very well, my dear, very well. Just as you think best. Let us leave that hymn until they are older.' And then he meanders away to talk to the children, leaving me feeling a bully and browbeater.

He drank his tea and then started up his car, setting off, very slowly and carefully, down the road to his vicarage.

The Pattern of the Afternoon

. . . Miss Clare and I served out slices of cold meat, mashed potatoes and salad, and Sylvia and Cathy and Anne carried them round. Miss Clare sat at the head of one table and I at the other, and when we had finished the first course two big boys, John and Ernest, cleared away. It was followed by plums and custard. Jimmy Waites was still rather awed by his new surroundings and ate very little, but Joseph Coggs, who, I suspected, very seldom had a dinner as well-prepared as this, ate a prodigious amount, coming up for a third helping of plums and custard with the older children. . . .

At a quarter-past one the children came back into their desks, breathless and cheerful, and after we had marked the register we tackled our joint composition again. After a while afternoon somnolence began to descend upon them, and when I thought they had studied the example of fair English, which they had been driven into producing, long enough, I went to the piano and we sang some of the songs which they had learnt the term before.

After play large sheets of paper were given out and the boxes of wax crayons; and the children were asked to illustrate either their day at the seaside or any other particular day that they had enjoyed during the past few weeks.

Industriously they set to work, blue crayons were scrabbled furiously along the bottom of the papers for the sea and yellow suns like daisies flowered on all sides. The room was quiet and happy, the afternoon sun beat in through the Gothic window and the clock on the wall stepped out its measured tread to home-time at half-past three.

As most of the children stay to dinner, and those that do go home live so very near, it seems wiser to have a short break at midday, start afternoon school early and finish early. In the summer this means that the children get a long spell of sunshine outdoors, and in the winter they can be safely home before it becomes dark.

We collected up our pictures and crayons and tidied up the room. The first day at school is always a long one, and the children looked sleepy.

The infants, who had been let out earlier, could be heard calling to each other as they ran up the road.

We stood and sang grace, wished each other 'Good afternoon' and made our way into the lobby. Jimmy and Joseph were standing there, anxiously waiting for Cathy.

'Did you enjoy school?' I asked them. Jimmy nodded.

'What about you, Joseph?'

'I liked the dinner,' he answered diplomatically in his husky gipsy voice. I left it at that.

Miss Clare was wheeling her bicycle across the playground. It struck me suddenly that she was looking old and tired.

She mounted carefully and rode slowly away down the road, upright and steady, but it seemed to me, as I stood watching her progress, that it needed more effort than usual; and this was only the first day of term.

How long, I wondered, would she be able to continue?

Comments

1. Good relationships with the children are shown in the opening sentence – not boasted about, but implicit in all their words and actions are trust and confidence. The children come readily to the teacher. They bring her things. They are confident enough to try to teach *her* (use of seaweed) and to argue with each other.

2. Miss Read is empathically aware of the self-consciousness of the new children. She tries to put Linda where she will be welcomed. Anne is made to feel important. The four young newcomers soon find safety.

3. The routine of Assembly is changed in the interests of settling in quickly.

4. Miss Read's care for the children is based on careful observation of details – Patrick's thumbsucking, cleanliness, nail-biting, scabies. Her treatment of nail-biters is positive and encouraging. She and Miss Clare work well together.

5. There is no suggestion that the children are 'naughty' because they are restless – it is accepted that it is the natural result of not having enough to do, and that it is the teacher's responsibility to see they are occupied. She appeals positively to them – and they 'assume a fierce air of trustworthiness'. Patrick is thrilled to be chosen.

6. Incidental teaching of left and right, as Patrick learns social competence.

7. At break Anne and Linda eat chocolate, and the newcomer is accepted as a friend. Details of Anne's home are well known to Miss Read. Cathy is accepting responsibility, not only for her little brother but for Joseph whose first day at school it is.

8. A happy school can exist in old buildings and primitive sanitary conditions.

9. The Vicar is welcomed with tea. Although Miss Read gets her way over the hymns, she does it tactfully and he accepts it. In how

many places would a similar incident be a source of continuing trouble?

10. School dinner really is the social and cooperative occasion that we are always being told it ought to be (but often isn't).

11. The afternoon's work passes gently and quietly. Everyone has plenty to do, but no one is harried along.

12. Jimmy has enjoyed his first day at school. Joseph is guarded, but Miss Read is acceptant and leaves it at that.

13. Solicitude shown for the welfare of her subordinate. Miss Clare had previously been described as having taught as an un-certificated teacher in the school for nearly forty years and having a most valuable knowledge of the children's families. 'She is now over sixty and her teaching methods have of late been looked upon by some visiting inspectors with a slightly pitying eye. They are, they say, too formal: the children should have more activity, and the classroom is unnaturally quiet for children of that age. This may be, but for all that, or perhaps because of that, Miss Clare is a very valuable teacher, for in the first place the children are happy, they are fond of Miss Clare, and she creates for them an atmosphere of serenity and quiet which means that they can work well and cheerfully.' This passage shows Miss Read look-ing positively all the time at Miss Clare's good qualities, not negatively at her limitations. She stresses and respects Miss Clare's integrity, the affection in which she is held, and the ex-cellent effect that this has on the children and on their ability to learn.

I hope that it will not be thought that I have gone into too much detail of underlining the obvious. It isn't all that obvious, for if it were, it would be more generally followed in practice than unfortunately it is. This seems to me a good clear example of excellent school morale and the passage – and indeed the whole book – is worthy of careful study. It survives close analysis far better than many a more pretentious educational tome, and there is much that we can learn from it. Under the deceptively simple writing is a wise account of how human relationships in school are developed and maintained. After the sections I have quoted the new children are pictured as returning to their homes, and their reactions to the day's events described.

Jimmy Waites lay on his lumpy flock mattress in a big brass bedstead which had once been his grandmother's.

As he lay there, sucking his thumb, drifting between sleeping and waking, the sights and sounds and smells of his first day at school crowded thick upon him. He saw the orderly rows of desks; some of them, including his own, had a twelve-inch square carved on to the lid, and he had enjoyed rubbing his fat forefinger along the grooves.

He remembered Miss Clare's soft voice; her big handbag and the little bottle of scent which she had taken from it. The top had rolled away towards the door and he had run to pick it up for her. She had dabbed a drop of cold scent into his palm for payment, but its fragrance had soon been lost in the ball of plasticine which he pummelled and rolled into buttons and marbles and, best of all, a long sinuous snake. He remembered the feel of it in his hand, dead, but horribly writhing as he swung it to and fro. Holding his stub of chalk, when he had tried to copy his letters from the blackboard, had not been so pleasurable. His fingers had clenched so tightly that they had ached.

He remembered the clatter of the milk bottles when the children returned them to the steel crate in the corner. He had enjoyed his milk largely because he had drunk it through a straw and this was new to him. It was gratifying to see the milk sink lower and lower in the bottle and to feel the cold liquid trickling down in his stomach.

He sighed, and wriggled down more closely into the lumpy mattress. Yes, he liked school. He'd have milk tomorrow with a straw, and play with plasticine snakes and perhaps go and see Cathy in the next room. Cathy . . . he was glad Cathy was there too. School was all very nice but there was nothing quite like home, where everything was old and familiar. Still sucking his thumb, Jimmy fell asleep.

Next door Joseph Coggs lay on a decrepit camp bed and listened to his parents talking downstairs. Their voices carried clearly up the stairs to the landing-bedroom, and he knew that his father was angry.

'Ninepence a day! Lot of nonsense! Pay four bob a week, near enough, for Joe's dinners alone? Not likely! You give 'un a bit o' bread and cheese same as you gives me, my girl.'

To Joseph, listening aloft, these were sad words, for although he too had dwelt on the new experiences of the day, as had the boy next door, and though the plasticine, milk bottles, desks and children had all made their lasting impression on his young mind, it was the dinner, warm and plentiful, the plums and, most of all, those three swimming platefuls of golden custard, that had meant most to young Joseph Coggs.

Two fat tears coursed down his face as, philosophically, he turned on his creaking bed and settled down to sleep.

Linda, in her new pale-blue bed in the little back bedroom was thinking about her new friend Anne. It was a pity she was so untidy; her mother would mind about that if she invited her to play one Saturday, but nevertheless she would do so. She liked this new school; the children had admired her frock and red shoes and she realized that she could queen it here far more easily than at the little private school which she had attended in Caxley. There had been too many other mothers of the same calibre as Mrs Moffat there, all vying with each other in dressing up their children and exhorting them to speak in refined voices. It had been an effort, Linda realized now, all the time. At the village school, despite her mother's warnings, she knew that she would be able to relax in the other children's company.

The thing that worried Linda most, as she looked back upon her first day at school, was the lavatories. She was appalled at this primitive sanitation.

It may be objected that this is not evidence, for Miss Read has moved from her position as chronicler of events in school to imaginary descriptions of what passes through the children's minds as they lie in bed before going to sleep. But the descriptions carry conviction and surely the point is that a good teacher who is well acquainted with the home backgrounds of the children in her care can very profitably spend some time in mentally putting herself in the place of certain children and considering what impact their experiences are having on them. By empathically asking herself, 'How would I like it if this happened to me?' she gets into the habit of trying to see things from their point of view, and so becomes more sensitized to social interrelationships. It sounds a simple prescription, but it is valuable none the less. Done on a large scale and systematically, it would get rid of many of the thoughtlessly wounding remarks that we all indulge in from time to time – 'You *would* say that, wouldn't you?' 'Can't you *ever* do anything sensible?' – whose effect can only be to increase insecurity and build up a negative self-picture, which presumably is the opposite of what we are intending to do. The unguarded remark can be damaging, and a great deal is to be learnt from the close study of what actually is said and done, though, as I have pointed out, it is more difficult to do this in a favourable, 'ordinary' context than in a dramatically unfavourable one.

★   ★   ★

I conclude that *Village School* and similar books are a valuable source from which to study the warp and woof of social relationships, perhaps all the more valuable because they describe normal situations unaffected by the presence of an outside observer. Sherif, for instance, in his studies of group behaviour and group identity (Sherif & Sherif, 1953), adopted the heroic expedient of disguising himself as caretaker of the building in order to explain his frequent appearances as observer! This carried its own artificiality, though it avoids the difficulty that children and teachers may behave more self-consciously when they are aware that they are being studied, as in some of the time-sampling researches.

In an attempt to get rid of the observer difficulty, I will take the next example from my own experience with adult students who were all experienced teachers. I was anxious to study the early stages of a situation, with a new group of students, to try to learn from day to day how interactions developed. So often we are dealing with already existent situations – the good morale of Village School, the bad morale of Towne – and it is important (though difficult) to try to trace the building up of group morale, good or bad, from its beginning. To some extent this was exemplified in Case study 1 The Joint Fieldwork Exercise, but the main part of this was unsatisfactory, and the latter part speculative, so there is a need for another example.

7 *From the Beginning*

(To make the pattern of interactions more comprehensible a simple form of coding has been adopted. Members of the new group whose settling–down process was being studied were given the names of colours, former students were named after trees, and staff members after fruit. Entries are made in diary form and comments will be given in parenthesis.)

Tuesday. On the first day that the new group met, Brown mentioned that Ash who came from the same district had phoned him last night and offered any help she could give. (He had met her casually for the first time three weeks before, so this was a helpful gesture on her part.)

Thursday. Plum and Date were both very satisfied by the good response of the students to the opening lectures.

Friday. Green said how pleased he had been to be accepted. He had been very impressed with work done in the schools by Beech and Elm.

Black said she had arranged to visit a school where Chestnut was working.

Blue – knows Oak and Pine well. Oak had helpfully arranged for her to do preliminary work for the course during the previous summer term. She was not applying for an impending headship because she preferred to take the course. White mentioned five old students he knew, who had all been very helpful – very impressed by their readiness to cooperate. He knew Willow very well – 'When he comes to lecture here to our group, I'll get them all to gang up against him! I hope we won't get fed up with each other before the end.' (Several students have got contacts who have presumably reassured them and helped them to settle down. 'Our group' indulging in solidarity is mentioned for the first time, but doubts are expressed about its permanence.)

Monday. Date had a long talk with Alder. In the holidays Alder had met Pink, who was full of fears, and tried to reassure him. 'I said – one of the things Date will tell you is that you can choose your line of work. You won't believe it, but it *is* true.' (Useful reinforcement of the official line. Students will often believe outsiders more easily than their own tutors.) 'I'm coming in at half term. I'll get our gang to make up a party and meet the present lot.' 'Ours was a good lot – at the end, our understanding was so close that it only needed one word and the others understood.' (Example of strong group feeling as an end-point to be gradually built up.)

Tuesday. Date (to whole group) – 'How do you feel after one week?'
A voice – 'Weak' (laughter).
Grey – 'Nervous'. Others laughed and he retracted his admission – 'Not really.'
Good response in lecture and didn't rush off at end.
(It is useful to explore feelings, and permit the expression of negative feelings.)

Thursday. Plum and Date both pleased with response – students very ready to join in. (Discussions are an excellent barometer of growing solidarity.) Nice easy interchange.

Monday. Grey knows Fir. Blue was absent ill, so sent in her paper on a joint project for someone else to read (even though she won't get the benefit of it, she won't hold up the group's work).

Tuesday. Willow's projected lecture went down well (no ganging up!) Purple invited him to the Union. Yellow said what a good lecture it had been (readiness to be appreciative).

Thursday. Green's enthusiasm at beginning of term (which perhaps was whistling in the dark) has cooled. He wants to transfer to another course, where he won't have to face an examination. Date temporized – don't decide too quickly, but if you feel you want to go, that will be quite all right.

Friday. Date phoned Chestnut (who lived near Green but didn't know him) and asked if he would be willing to help Green make up his mind. Also phoned Birch (a co-religionist) similarly. Both agreed. Black had enjoyed her visit to Chestnut. She said she was helping the other students in the hostel with her to settle down. (Small tendrils of positive actions being sent out towards others. Tutor takes responsibility of initiating help in impending crisis with Green.)

X, *Tuesday*. Alder, Elder, and two more old students came in to evening lecture – all off to Union together at end; plus members of new group. Green (helped by Chestnut and Birch) made up his mind to stay. (It is usually a wise move to leave a door open so that people do not feel trapped. If they are reassured that they can go, they often decide to stay, and the decision is then their own, and their morale is helped.)

Thursday. A group of students sat on at the end of a seminar, ready to talk. (Growing confidence in each other.) Much more open about feelings of uncertainty and strain – 'a help to know others feel the same', 'put off by how much others know'. Date suggested that if they were worried about expectations, they might ask old students. 'We have – that man in the Union on Tuesday' (Alder).

Red: '*He* was very worried last year when he came to visit our school.'

Yellow: 'But he's enjoying the course very much *now*!' (laughter). (A further example of how useful interactions across the years can be. Alder's word will be believed because he, like them, had been worried and uncertain.)

Monday. Eight students very impressed by the work Larch is doing.

Tuesday. Plum said the students very much enjoyed a talk given by Maple, and had eaten out of her hand. Date asked permission to enter the students' common-room to see White and Purple, and got an impression of a very cheerful band. The caretaker commented what a very nice group they were. (A most valuable and perceptive informant. As Sherif knew, caretakers see a lot!) White and Purple agreed very pleasantly when Date altered arrangements for them, though they were inconvenienced. At the end of last lecture, the whole group left the building in a noisy whoosh – pulling the secretary's leg, rallying the caretaker, Maple, Plum, and Date. (Laughter is a most useful social cement.)

Thursday. Mauve was odd one out – he wanted one thing, rest another. Mauve also critical of lectures. Brown looked squashed. (Examples of unfavourable reactions in growing group solidarity.)

By this time, five weeks had elapsed, the group had settled down well, and the detailed notes of interactions were discontinued, except for one last note three weeks later. On the phone Elder said the group was most cooperative, and ready to ensure the success of some carols he was arranging for the end of term. When asked how he knew this, it went back to X, the evening in the Union more than a month previously with a very mixed and heterogeneous collection! Of such trifling experiences is morale built up.

When we look back over these notes, the most striking thing is the large part played in the settling-in process by former students. Tutors are not always aware how many contacts there are between students and their predecessors even on a one-year course and may be surprised that this is a factor to be taken into account when considering how students come to terms with their new lot. Teachers will be less surprised, because for them it is obvious that new children entering a school will have contacts with older friends and siblings, and will enter with attitudes and expectations already formed to some extent. It therefore becomes a matter of importance how these predecessors have perceived their experience. Do they condemn it? Do they value it, but honestly admit that there were tough and anxious stretches? Do they excessively praise it? On the whole, the middle reaction is to be hoped for, for the over-enthusiast may be donning a defensive cloak to hide from himself his own anxieties. Since these are inevitably evoked by entering on a course, perhaps all the more so when members are adults, it is more helpful to the newcomer if his mentor can admit to having felt the same tensions and rivalries as he does himself. It is not all honey settling down in a new group, and even in a generally helpful group, individuals will have their moments of feeling lost and out of step (compare for example the entries concerning Mauve and Brown. Here I may say that Brown gained confidence steadily. Mauve took longer to be fully integrated but eventually became so.) Much is to be gained, in all-round honesty and openness, by giving students opportunities to express their uncertainties and to say frankly when they feel unsure, rather than expecting them always to maintain a façade of cheerful competence. Naturally one hopes that the predominating tone of a group will be positive and cheerful!

*   *   *

To follow on from this example, it may be useful to give views expressed by Grey (who admitted to nervousness and then retracted it defensively) in a long talk with Plum a year later. Looking back, he was able to admit to ambivalent attitudes, and his retrospective view is valuable for this reason. It gives a clear picture of factors that increase and reduce morale both in individuals and in the group as a whole. The account here is transcribed from full notes taken by Plum at the time, and, as before, comments are in parenthesis.

8 In Retrospect

Grey began by asking about the other members of his group, how they were, and what had been heard of them; and also expressed interest in the current group and how they were settling. He asked whether it was helpful to Plum and Date to have the views of students looking back, and, being assured that it was, began to talk. At several points in his practical work he had been so discouraged that he felt like giving up, but he had learned a lot from it and was still learning.

Getting to know people made a difference to discussion and made possible the feeling of a united group that he had experienced. Smaller groupings helped here – going in twos and threes on visits, contacting individuals over items presented in lecture or seminar, meal-time conversations, and so on.

Discussion – early on he was bored with the long-winded papers others presented and felt it would have been better if the pattern had been as it was at the end just before the examination – a short relevant statement and then well-chosen questions to consider. Looking back, however, he realized they would not have been able to do this at that stage. (In other words, learning to discuss is a developing process. Students become technically more capable of discussion as time goes on. Discussion helps group feeling, and, equally, a positive group feeling makes discussion and therefore learning easier.)

He described the pre-examination period as free, comfortable, spontaneous, really listening to others, taking a share though not necessarily saying a lot, relaxed. He put this down to security within the group, with acceptance and affection at quite a deep level felt for the others, and a genuine wish to hear what others had to say. (Many people will rub their eyes at this as a description of the time immediately preceding an examination, but it has been independently confirmed to me by Puce of this group, and by members of other groups. Granted that in common experience the very reverse of this is often true, yet high morale of this nature *can* be achieved.)

Ideas – during the year people's ideas grew closer together and a body of agreed ideas was built up so that they couldn't see how things could be thought of differently. He was surprised on return to his school to find other people not in agreement, for somehow he had expected their ideas to have changed as well as his own! (Compare a similar statement made by Alder about close understanding. It is obvious that this is a situation with potentialities for ill or for good, depending whether the consensus has been achieved by indoctrination, when it becomes akin to brainwashing, or by free discussion and the encouragement of independent thought.)

As far as work was concerned, at first there was a good deal of anxiety about standards and about the amount expected; and jokes with an anxious undercurrent were made about being assessed on written and verbal contributions. Every individual wanted to do well, and Yellow, who was outstandingly able, caused the others much worry. He did so much, and knew so much – but the others didn't feel too badly about it because everyone recognized his sincerity. Plum commented that Grey seemed to feel Yellow couldn't help it and couldn't be *blamed* for it!! (This is an interesting point, the potential isolation of an outstanding member from the rest of the group. In this case, jealousies and rivalries do not seem to have developed as they might have done.) Grey said that students were concerned about tutors' appraisals at the beginning of the year, but at the end they were more interested in the approval of the group, and less concerned about tutors' assessments – in spite of the forthcoming examinations. (Another interesting point. It shows the strength of group sanctions, and, again, this is something which could be used constructively or destructively. An unhappy and inharmonious group in which backbiting is rife can cause much unhappiness to individuals, just because the desire for group approval is so strong, while a healthy group can give security to its members.)

Even early on, he said, congratulations were given to people who made a useful contribution – this started with perhaps one person commending, then two or three, and later on everyone commented freely on what was helpful. (Positive attitudes grow gradually, and with them grows a feeling of security, that it is safe to relax and rely on other people's goodwill: as opposed to the tense, wary, suspicious watchfulness of a group that is torn with rivalries and split into opposing camps, where unfavourable comments can be expected and where no relaxation or self-revealing statement can possibly be risked. In the latter setting it is unwise to do too well, or you may expose yourself to envious comments from the group that you are teacher's pet, etc. – there is an incalculable amount of underfunctioning due to this. In contrast where the group feeling is helpful and positive, individuals are encouraged to achieve to their maximum potential, often to their own surprise as well as to that of everyone else.)

★   ★   ★

These last two examples should be taken together for they are complementary. I should add that the group concerned was a fairly average group and though this is the only occasion on which I have been able to study the development of group feeling from its earliest beginnings, the findings and relationships could have been paralleled with a number of other groups. I suggest that we are too easily ready to accept a low standard in group behaviour as inevitable, and that much more harmony can be achieved than some people think possible. Just as there is much individual underfunctioning, so, also there is much *group* underfunctioning, to the detriment both of happiness and of efficient and creative learning.

This leads on to a related point, that many situations are, so to speak, neutral. If they are part of a context where there is already a lot of trouble, they will be taken negatively, and result in further trouble, but if they are part of a more favourable context, they are more likely to be taken positively. This will be the theme of my next example.

9 *Things can go either Way*

Some new educational films, of interest to geographers, were ordered for a college of education. The head of the geography department had previously told his students about the films and they had expressed interest in seeing them, but unfortunately by the time they arrived it was only a few days before their final examinations. Three films, each lasting nearly an hour, are a time-consuming addition to a revision programme already stretched to its limit. It was true that the films were interesting, useful, and could be regarded as relaxation, but coming at a bad time like this they could cause annoyance among the students, and increase anxiety and tension rather than a release of pressure. The lecturer decided, after careful consideration, that he would show the films one a day at the end of the afternoon, and make it quite clear that attendance was voluntary. After each film there was a discussion, which was kept factual and pointed, and which ended in ten minutes. In the event two-thirds of the students (not the same ones all the time) stayed for the films and no undue tensions were aroused.

This is not an example of the *gaining* of morale: it is an example of how high morale, already existing in a group, can affect favourably the group's perception of situations that with another less integrated group could cause considerable discontent and ill-feeling.

'Why all this *now*?' 'We've had all this extra pushed on to us', 'However can we cope with all the work?' are predictable reactions to the situation. It is true that the lecturer made no effort to enforce attendance, which would certainly have created a grievance, but it is worth noting that merely to *say* attendance was voluntary would not in itself have been sufficient to avert trouble. In a group with low morale, where there is no real trust in the staff, suspicions would merely have been aroused ('Does he mean it?' 'It probably means these topics come in the examination so we *must* go', 'You'll fail if you don't', etc.). The already existing poor spirit is reinforced, and the evidence is twisted in accordance with the group's suspicious perceptions. So the geography lecturer, looking back on the incident, was right to feel that he had been lucky in his group. 'What a nice lot they are!' would probably sum up his reactions, and a virtuous spiral of pleasant appreciation between lecturer and students ensues, very different from the vicious spiral that the same events could have caused in less happy circumstances.

But things don't just happen; they are caused, complex as the causation may be. What makes this field so difficult is the apparent variation in effects that the 'same events' can have – unfortunate or fortunate – depending largely on the pre-existent state of morale in the group. This is always a factor which must be taken into calculation, and this example shows clearly that a group's perceptions and expectations can influence the outcome. The lecturer behaved fairly sensibly in that (1) he kept it voluntary, (2) he was present at the films and took the discussions himself, thus sharing the inconvenience with his students, (3) he found a happy medium with his discussion – he neither had none, which could have seemed perfunctory and wouldn't have used the films as valuably as possible, nor went on squeezing the last drop of utility, to the students' impatience, (4) he considered carefully the students' point of view and avoided the most obvious traps. But sensible behaviour of this sort in the lecturer is not enough: it may be a necessary condition, but it is not a sufficient condition. Into every situation he trails 'clouds of glory' which are the result of his reputation slowly built up over a period of time and which largely influence his group's readiness to take a dim view, or a favourable view, as the case may be, of his current activities. Some causes are lost before ever they are even started.

Another example from a different field can make the same point. An inexperienced teacher is having a hard time with her class of juniors. They are not exactly out of hand, but things are not going well. So when she suggests a new activity she is disappointed by the tepid reaction she receives. A similar suggestion made to the same class by a popular teacher with all the prestige of many successes behind her would be much more favourably received. How unfair! yet how natural. In each case an essential element in the situation is the group's perceptions of it. In one case they are prepared to cooperate, in the other case they are not. I am not simply making the point that there is a difference of *discipline* (it is not just that in one case the children comply from fear – because they don't) the difference goes deeper than that, and the quality of active cooperation that the popular and successful teacher evokes is one of her most valuable attributes – a bonus, shall we say, for good work over a period. The young teacher's problems are not *merely* ones of discipline, though this is probably what she is most conscious of. But even if she had no difficulty in the actual management of the children, she would still be faced with a lack of active cooperation, which the other teacher gets, apparently without effort. It is this last phrase 'apparently without effort' which seems so unfair to the young teacher. It all looks so easy! Nothing succeeds like success, and a habit of success, built up over a time, is a great morale-raiser, both for teacher and for children.

★   ★   ★

So, by devious routes, we have come to the back of the Gorgon's head. The fatal word 'discipline' has been raised, and the issue can no longer be postponed. What do we mean when we say that a teacher has 'good discipline'? I put this question in an examination to a number of teachers, who answered in writing, without any opportunity for reflection (so that the replies tap their unstudied reactions) and without any chance to consult others (so that they are not contaminated by majority opinion).

10 Teachers' Views on Discipline

Each statement will be given, and then followed by my comments.

Mrs A

A teacher has good discipline when he has the full cooperation of his class, and is able to steadily and progressively help them develop along those lines which he has carefully considered to be the best suited to their individual needs.

*   *   *

Succinct summary, but raises some essential points.

1. Emphasis on cooperation.

2. Discipline is progressive and should develop with the children.

3. Different individuals have different needs.

4. Need for thoughtful consideration, i.e. not just rule of thumb.

Mr B

The main point to aim at is to involve the children in the whole organization of the classroom. It is necessary to establish good relations with the children, and to realize that each individual in the classroom is different and attempt to cater for these differences.

In considering the 'involvement of children in the classroom organization', thought must be given to seating arrangements. Personally, I like the children to choose their friends and sit together in groups. Then the various questions of duties and responsibilities for classroom organization must be decided between the children and the teacher. The feeling of 'this is our classroom', 'we must keep it tidy ourselves' must be present.

In establishing good relations with the children, the teacher must understand, or try to understand, their needs and genuinely care for them, respecting them, and give a true impression that he trusts them. That, of course, is not enough, for disciplinary problems can arise because the work is not suitable for the child. It is vital therefore, that the work given must not be too hard, too easy, or dull and uninteresting: ample opportunity must be given to each child to follow a particular interest in order that he may be happy and successful.

There must be room for spontaneity, freedom of movement, and, of course, order and routine must be present. Controlled freedom is perhaps a paradox, but licence is disastrous. Rules there must be, but a teacher will, if he is wise, discuss the need for rules so that the children will understand why the rules are necessary. Firmness and consistency will be expected from the teacher, there is no need for softness.

I conclude therefore, that a teacher has good discipline when he has the support of his class, when the children are trying to practise self-discipline, when they are working on interesting work suitable and graded to their abilities and interests, and finally when he trusts them and takes them all into his confidence for the important task of living and learning together.

*　　　*　　　*

Some important suggestions are made – the need for the children to cooperate in discipline for it to be valuable, with the emphasis on developing self-control; the importance of the teacher's organization and technical skill in providing suitable work for the children; and the need for trust and mutual confidence between teacher and children. There is also a very interesting point about the feeling of 'belonging' and 'involvement' – the teacher who manages to inspire in children a feeling that they belong is not likely to have many disciplinary problems.

Mr C

The child needs to have limits set for him. He needs to know what is permissible and what is not permissible. The child has to experiment and find his way in the world so may go to extremes to see if it affects the all-important relationship between himself and parent, himself and teacher, and himself and classmates. If the child steps outside these limits it is usually because his developing self-control has broken down and he is crying out for help. He requires additional help in the form of external controls to help him through the 'sticky' patch.

Children who behave badly more often need help rather than punishment. The set limits, however, should be adhered to. If punishment is needed it should be given, but the child must understand why he is being punished and must be shown when it has been given that the relationship is as it was before.

★   ★   ★

1. Limits are necessary.

2. Unreasonable to expect children to control themselves all the time, hence need for external controls.

3. Positive attitude – children need help rather than punishment – but at the same time realistic and not airy-fairy. Need for understanding and reassurance.

Mrs D

Many years ago I worked in a so-called 'tough school'. One lady member of the staff interested me very much because, when supervising the children's dinner-time, she was able to enforce complete silence upon at least 200 children. The meal usually lasted about twenty minutes and during that time no child spoke. This was the rule of the school, other teachers had difficulty in enforcing it, especially me, but Miss X did it with apparently no effort at all. It was the same in her classroom, where about forty-five ten-year-olds sat in their desks and worked in complete silence. It worried me somewhat that I was unable to do this, especially as the headmistress remarked regularly about the lack of discipline in my classroom, but I didn't really see anything wrong in allowing the children to talk quietly during a handwork lesson or to ask a friend to pass the blotting paper during arithmetic. However, being very young, I did not argue with authority and did my best to imitate Miss X. When she had a nervous break-down, a supply teacher took over my class for a term and I went into Miss X's classroom expecting the worst. It was so bad that I nearly walked out and gave up teaching. Looking back, I cannot think why I stayed unless it was a stubborn streak in me that was determined not to give in. Miss X must have controlled those forty-five children by sheer force of will-power, and once she had gone they just ran wild. It was terrible. The headmistress came in several times a day to tell me to keep the class quiet, and it took me over a month to restore some sort of order and seemly behaviour. I did it by the only method I could think of – providing them with so much written work that no one had time to make much noise. The school was unstreamed so I had five groups with a very wide range of ability. At times I wondered if I, too, would retire with a nervous breakdown. I remember that I did no oral work during that first month and my first oral lesson with them, once they had calmed down and become accustomed to me, resulted in complete chaos once more – and another visit from the headmistress. By the end of that term, however, I felt I was in control of the situation, the atmosphere had become much more pleasant and friendly towards me, and the children towards each other, and they had accepted my ruling that it was permitted to whisper to one's neighbour but to no one else because it wasn't fair to disturb other people who were busy. Miss X did not return and I handed the class over to a large cheerful man who had just left the army and done one year's training, and he managed them very well.

Now, Miss X, according to the opinion of the headmistress, had 'good discipline' and I more or less accepted the fact that I did not have 'good discipline', although I never quite understood how it was that my children made progress comparable with the children in other classes if I had this big flaw in my ability as a teacher. As one of the mothers said, "'E's ever so 'appy with you, Miss; you 'it 'im if 'e don't behave!' I went on for years not understanding until about five years ago I met a retired H.M.I. who said that the true test of discipline was how the children behaved when the teacher went out of the classroom for about ten minutes, and it suddenly came to me that this old man was right, the discipline must, in the end, come from the children themselves. They must learn to control themselves so that they can behave and work quietly even when the teacher is not watching them, for this is what they must learn to do in adult life – to be trusted to work without constant supervision. How can this be encouraged? Firstly, I think that every child should be given work which is at the correct level for his age and ability, a clever child who is not 'stretched' will become bored and amuse himself by distracting others. Similarly, Bill, with an IQ of about 75, will give up trying to do work that is too difficult for him to understand, and he too, is likely to disturb the other children. So the work for each child must be carefully graded and, secondly and equally important, each child should know what he has to do and where to find the next step, and, if the teacher is busy or is called away, the brighter children should be encouraged to help their fellows who need a little explanation; this graded individual work is, I think, essential in reading, writing, and in number. Thirdly, I have always found it very useful to permit children who really are 'stuck' to finish off a painting or continue with some handwork, until the teacher is free to attend to them, always provided of course that the classroom is arranged so that this can take place without disturbing other children. So everyone has plenty to do. Children enjoy being busy and I believe that a contented occupied child is seldom a nuisance. They are members of their own group, respected and respecting others, respecting their need for privacy and quietness and respecting their property. This surely is good preparation for their adult life. But in adult life there is always someone in authority over us, whether it is the factory foreman or the bishop, and we must all submit to the laws of the land in which we live. So the children must learn to live within the discipline of the class-teacher in their own room and within the general overall discipline of the head-master. There must be some rules, there must be some boundaries, within which the children know they must stay, but it should be possible to keep these rules down to a minimum; however, they must be there to give the children a sense of security and safety. I have come a long way since I worried about Miss X and my 'lack of discipline' – now I am too busy thinking about the children in my class and I find that I tend to take the discipline for granted – when I have time I'll think about that.

*　　*　　*

Example of differing ways of class control. The young teacher no doubt made mistakes through sheer inexperience, but the children, though troublesome, were on her side – "'e's ever so happy with you Miss'. The older woman made it a battle which, though she won at the time, ended tragically in her ultimate defeat – she drove herself as well as the children 'by sheer will-power' beyond all reason. The 'large cheerful man' was no doubt helped by being large! i.e. there was an element of fear in the children's reaction to him which may not have been a bad thing. The main point, however, was that his attitudes and cheerfulness were positive. The head doesn't come very well out of this example. She seems to have endorsed the older woman's approach, without sensing the strain and the risks taken. Presumably she was responsible for the rule of silence at meals which, not surprisingly, caused general difficulty in enforcement. She was critical of the young teacher without, as far as is mentioned, offering any positive help or guidance, but contenting herself with visits of reproof, i.e. she played a purely repressive role towards both teacher and children. She doesn't seem to have increased her help when the young teacher moved to the difficult class, or to have given any praise when the young teacher gradually won through. In openly commenting on the teacher's 'poor' discipline she sapped her confidence in a way that might, but fortunately didn't, have had lasting effects. One wonders how many other young teachers have, in fact, given up teaching because of similar difficulties and mishandling? We must remember of course that she *might* have given help, but 'no help' was how it felt to the young teacher. Towards the end of the extract the teacher gives her own, mature, views on what constitutes good discipline, with the emphasis positively on keeping the children happily and interestingly occupied with suitable and well-graded work, and a recognition that in the last resort self-control is what matters, though it may have to be supplemented by external controls until the children are able to manage the more difficult objective.

Miss E

I recall my own problems with class control during my early teaching days. Two periods of scripture with thirty children were a problem. Eventually I decided we would make news sheets covering in a familiar form the period of the Old Testament I was supposed to be expounding. My problem disappeared – apparently. These thirteen- and fourteen-year-old boys took to the work, started bringing in books from the library, and cooperated with one another in writing and illustrating. Two boys went off with jars to fetch paint water, and came back accompanied by the deputy head. 'You'll have to stop this work,' she said. 'We can't have boys wandering around the corridor.' I tried to put my point of view, but was just told, 'No, you can't do this sort of thing until you've got good discipline.' I gathered that I must first make my pupils submissive, and then I could let them have a little enjoyment.

The relationship between the teacher and the pupils is the important factor in discipline in whichever form one sees it. Sometimes it is deliberately created by a certain amount of fear of the teacher. This can produce an atmosphere in which certain pupils will absorb all they are being taught, and can also result in a quiet atmosphere that helps those who work in a certain way. However, there are many children who will not be able to learn in such conditions. Also this kind of enforced behaviour will be unlikely to lead to the type of personal development and eventual self-discipline which we hope to see.

From enforced discipline one might be able to lead on to the more relaxed atmosphere that is more conducive to genuine learning. I have frequently heard the advice given that one should be over-strict at first so that the children will know that they cannot take liberties. Another teacher will tell you, 'Hold them tight in this class. If you give them an inch they will take a yard.' You may succeed in holding them, but perhaps the only reason that they grab for 'a yard' is because they have so rarely been given 'an inch'.

I think the only teacher who really can be said to have good discipline is the one whose pupils behave as they do willingly. He probably won't have a still and silent class very often, and others may think that he allows pupils to be too familiar. However, their willing cooperation is probably founded on an interest in what they are doing, or at least an understanding of why they are doing it. I think it is also the result of a certain respect for the teacher as a person, because he has allowed them to get to know him sufficiently well instead of remaining on his pedestal. Because of their interest in what they are learning and because of their security in their relationship to the teacher, they are disciplining themselves.

★　　★　　★

Again an example of two contrasting views on discipline – the deputy head's legalistic and unimaginative, based on a jaundiced view of time-wasting activities, though no doubt sensible in the first instance as far as it went; and the youngster with more of the root of the matter, the essence of teaching, in her, blissfully unaware of the (quite genuine) snags and difficulties that were all the deputy saw. What *is* a youngster to do who has a difficult subject like Scripture to take with 3C? If they are bored, they will be troublesome, and then she will have to suppress them. The deputy's wisdom in the end leads to a blinder alley than the youngster's risky choice, for the road marked 'Suppression' leads nowhere, while there is always the hope that the youngster, having acquired caution and know-how, will develop into one who can see that 'the only teacher who really has good discipline is the one whose pupils behave as they do willingly'.

Mr F

There should be a reasonably common level. If there is great difference and unbalance, other teachers feel the brunt, particularly where children move from class-teacher to class-teacher. If Mr A is extremely strict, 'noses down and not a murmur', Miss B will feel it next lesson when they go to her. A uniformity is desirable.

Where will this come from? The head, if wise, will have discussed the problem and what the aims of the school should be. The staff, able to put their point of view, will have drawn up a core of a good standard of behaviour expected throughout the school at all times of the day. If discussed in this way, the staff will feel they have a say in the general running of the school and that they are not just complying with the head's whims and fancies.

What is the teacher's attitude towards the children, both in and out of class? Are they considered friends or just 'those little devils I've got'. Inside school is the teacher willing to open a door for a child; if a cup is returned during break by a child, is it shown courtesy? Little things do matter where children are concerned; a child knows whether he is somebody or nobody.

★   ★   ★

In addition to points that have been previously commented on, this teacher raises the important point of equalizing the expectations of different members of staff, preferably through democratic discussion rather than a fiat from the head.

Mr G

My very early experiences in teaching were none too happy in the matter of keeping good discipline, and were in common, I suppose, with those of many other young and inexperienced teachers. A friend, who taught in the same school, was fortunate in not being troubled in this respect, and I can remember asking him: 'How do you manage it?' – expecting, no doubt, some magic formula that would banish all cares. His reply, disappointingly, was: 'I just don't allow it.' Well, nor did I want to allow 'it', I suppose, but it didn't work for me.

*   *   *

This raises an interesting point. Not only is there no magic remedy which when imparted solves everything, but the same remedies applied by different teachers have different effects. Children seem to have an instinctive calculus as to what they can get away with, so the 'large cheerful man' of the earlier example *started off* at an advantage as compared with the young girl. This advantage is not necessarily maintained into maturity, but it is important in the first instance in setting teachers off confidently or unconfidently.

Mr H

The important thing was not the immediate effect of the teacher's technique but the effect that it had on the children generally. So often I had observed a class of children kept sitting silently in their desks most of the day, only to go wild when let out into the playground for a PE lesson with me. They also seemed so antagonistic towards each other. It struck me that this method of impressive discipline was designed to cater more for the teacher's needs than for those of the children.

Now that I had decided that the aim should be to gain discipline among the children by catering for their needs, I wondered how it could be done in the situation. When Douglas (a thirteen-year-old boy in my class who had been separated from his parents) punched the other children and refused to work, it almost seemed the natural thing to shout at him and force him to work. But reading the school records of the boy, I realized how often this technique had failed – and perhaps even contributed to his present condition. When Douglas was given a special task, designed to suit his ability and interests – cutting pictures from comics and making up stories for the tape-recorder, he seemed a different boy and I was pleased to realize that the change – if even perhaps at this stage temporary – was coming from within him and was not imposed by me.

My definition of a teacher that has good discipline would be as follows:

(i) He should have personal good self-discipline so that the influence of his character and personality is a good one.

(ii) He should aim at a child-centred approach, by seeing the children's needs, and look for the causes of bad behaviour rather than for an immediate way of stopping it.

(iii) He should be aware that much bad behaviour in a school is caused by a badly designed curriculum and poor methods of organization.

(iv) He should be aware that children are generally truly better behaved in a calm, friendly situation with happy relationships with a teacher who is respected and in turn respects the children.

(v) He should not try to be superhuman and should recognize that feelings such as anger arise occasionally and are sometimes well deserved. It is good also for the children to see a real whole personality and not a classroom-acted one.

★　　★　　★

There are several valuable new points here

1. Children who are unduly kept down become aggressive towards each other.

2. A distinction is made between discipline based on the children's needs and that which considered only the teacher's needs and convenience.

3. Look for the causes of bad behaviour rather than just stopping it. (We saw this also in the earlier case study about Towne School.)

4. The teacher should try to be a real person, and trust his spontaneity, rather than bottle up his genuine reactions in an attempt to do the socially accepted right thing. Paradoxically, by a display of temper which is 'real' he may achieve more contact than by a cold virtuous façade which is felt to be phoney. This is not, however, to advocate a continuous display of temper!

Mr I

To bring together my thoughts I would say a teacher has good discipline if:

1. He is respected by the children – that is, that code of conduct which he desires is looked upon as just and fair, and for the good and pleasure of all.

2. The children are happy as a result of a feeling of security. They know just how far they can go.

3. Behaviour in the classroom is orderly, busy, and with some chatter. I always suspect the deathly quiet classroom.

*   *   *

Lays stress on respect, security, and happiness. A balanced order is maintained – no suggestion of *laissez-faire*.

Mr J

Discipline begins in a good relationship with the child or children concerned. Even in the home (perhaps particularly in the home) and with corporal punishment, this holds true; for punishment, of whatever sort, if it is to be effective must be seen by the child as a temporary withdrawal of esteem or affection by a loved or admired adult. Lacking this characteristic it becomes an interference with an individual's liberty, an unwarranted act of aggression which in itself may justify in the child's eyes the use of aggression by him towards the environment in return at some later date, or a quite ludicrous action bringing the punishing adult into disrepute in his eyes.

Nevertheless, discipline is not just a matter of punishment. Indeed, one could say the better the discipline a teacher possesses, the less does he or she resort to punishment.

Neither is discipline merely a matter of 'keeping them down', 'keeping quiet', or 'keeping their noses to the grindstone', etc. etc.

Rather does it lie in the establishing of codes of conduct and behaviour which all approve and, for the most part, observe for the good of all.

Noise, bustle, activity, and so on are not inconsistent with good discipline, indeed they presuppose it.

The mutual respect of teacher and class is important, and the teacher who secretly despises his charges can hardly be surprised if he finds himself faced with behaviour problems.

When work is gauged at the children's level, and catches their interest because by means of it they are able to visualize themselves achieving their own goals in ways that to them are socially significant then trouble is far less likely to occur. Even then it is necessary for the teacher so to arrange the situation that unnecessary causes of friction and frustration are avoided. In a craft period, for example, one would not present the child with materials or tools that were unsuitable for the job in hand (e.g. clay which is too soggy) or that were unsuited to his age-level (e.g. too childish). Nor would one put him to work with someone with whom he particularly cannot get on, for I have found that the structure of one's grouping can have a profound significance for discipline.

Difficulties also may have an internal cause, which brings me to a point I have not yet considered – that of ascertaining the cause of a child's indiscipline. It is here that good discipline will be seen to go hand in hand with the careful keeping and wise use of records. These will assist the teacher to determine (if not finally at least provisionally) possible cause of disturbance. It is necessary, for example, to distinguish between the healthy naughtiness of the normal boy, the naughtiness that is 'a cry for help' and is indicative of some underlying personal problem, and the naughtiness that is indicative of something lacking in the child's experience or environment. These three forms of naughtiness will not be given the same treatment and the teacher will also do her best to see that she is not too easily satisfied with explanations that are no explanation (e.g. that the child is lazy) but merely descriptions of behaviour.

The teacher who aspires to good discipline will also need to be well aware of the individual differences in her children and of the stage of development each has reached. She will not expect, for example, the behaviour 'appropriate' to a ten-year-old simply because he has lived through ten chronological years. She will avoid the trouble consequent upon expecting too much too early from a physically large but slow-developing boy. She will be like-wise sympathetic towards the child who is going through a 'bad patch' at home or who is facing other difficulties.

Nevertheless she will 'use' the characteristics of the develop-mental level that her charges have reached. She will know, for example, that infants will do anything to gain her approval but she will not use this weapon to a too great, and possibly damaging, extent.

She will know that adolescents respond (usually) to reason – granted of course the always necessary good relationships – and to a chance to help run things themselves, but she will avoid the temptation to 'use' the adolescent's concern for what his peers think, for this would tend to foster a critical approach to others which this teacher would wish to avoid and replace by an accepting attitude.

Like a balanced curriculum, then, good discipline depends in large measure upon taking account of the children's individual needs and differences.

★   ★   ★

This extract goes into greater detail than the others on the different reactions of individuals making up the class and the need for individualized treatment both in work and in behaviour, but the underlying principles are similar to those expressed in previous papers.

H

Mr K

True discipline comes from within and a teacher with really good discipline in his classroom will have the children's trust, respect, and in some cases love.

This kind of teacher–pupil relationship *can* be achieved but it will never be reached by a policy of *laissez-faire* or brute force. It requires a good understanding of the children by the teacher in the first place. Careful observation of the children, getting to know the children's likes and dislikes.

Children need security, someone they can trust and respect and someone who is emotionally sound. They cannot trust a teacher who is never the same for two days running, they do not know what to expect.

With good motivation, active participation in class and school work, a fair, stable teacher, and mutual trust and respect between the teacher and the pupils, you can say that a teacher has good discipline.

*　　*　　*

As in previous extracts, the emphasis is on positive qualities – trust, affection, fairness.

I have chosen these extracts because they all in different ways emphasize the positive qualities inherent in the idea of 'discipline', so that punishment for infractions is not allowed to usurp the centre of the stage. It may be objected that they are a biased selection, but, if so, they are no more biased than the usual treatment of discipline in teachers' utterances at conferences and elsewhere, and it is about time that the balance was redressed. It can be helpful to look at the other side of the coin for a change, particularly since it is possible to escape the usual stultifying and negative approach in favour of one that offers more chance of helping us to escape the impasse of suppression – resentment – resistance – more suppression. None of the teachers live in cloud-cuckoo-land or believe in *laissez-faire*; they agree that limits must be set and maintained, and that the security of children as well as teachers is helped by such limits; they are not iconoclastic – but in the last resort they see that 'discipline' is not an end in itself and is only to be valued in terms of its consequences in promoting the positive and harmonious development of individuals in society which is what we mean by education.

Part Two · Principles

Introduction

The thesis of this book can now be stated simply: it will be amplified in succeeding chapters.

A situation of poor morale is characterized by:
- suspicion
- tension
- frustration
- underfunctioning
- poor relationships, both among peers and towards authority figures.

A situation of good morale is characterized by:
- feelings of trust
- relaxation
- happiness
- effective learning
- productiveness
- good relationships, both within the group and spreading outwards from it, and including respect for authority that is not merely based on fear.

Discipline is best approached via the study of morale, so that the emphasis is placed not just on coercive battles to maintain a semblance of order, but on reasonable and willing cooperation. Schools benefit by having an orderly framework, which may sometimes in this imperfect world have to be enforced by sanctions and penalties, but the orderly framework is not an end in itself. Thus, for example, school uniform has its uses, but if it leads to an unending series of battles the game is not worth the candle, for the more important things have already slipped away and been lost. The real question to ask is whether the child is proud of his school, his class, and himself; and, if he is not, how he can become so.

Good morale is important not only because it is pleasanter, but also because it is conducive to more and better work and learning. A happy atmosphere in which scholars and students on the one hand, and staff on the other feel free to be themselves is also one in which they have space to grow and in which they can learn. An incalculable amount of underfunctioning can be attributed directly to personal and social unsureness: it is safer not to take the initiative, but simply to conform with known expectations. In an accepting social climate this drag on performance is released and the 'social learning' that takes place is positive, not negative.

Finally, we need to be clear what are the important issues and not be side-tracked down minor channels. All the de-streaming in the world, for example, will do no good if the devaluation of the slow learner so often implicit in the much-criticized C stream still continues in the new system – it will simply have shifted the problem into a new organizational form. The crux is in the attitudes of teachers and parents to children who are failing in school, and in the attitudes these children themselves acquire as a result of their experiences.

So I make no apology for considering morale the most neglected educational question of our age.

I *The Morale of Individuals*

Morale has naturally been most fully studied in the context of war and in the operations of the armed forces. To a lesser extent the reactions of civilian populations, usually in a setting of violence, have been the subject of study e.g. the Leighton's and OSS researches into the morale of American civilians in World War II. Morale in schools has been much less considered, and usually only in cases where dramatic and disturbing infractions of order have occurred, and official inquiries have been set up – for example, after the fatal shooting at Standon Farm Approved School – or periodic allegations of brutally excessive 'disciplining' of culprits. The well-known inquiry into the attitudes of teachers towards the use of corporal punishment in schools showed a confused and confusing state of public opinion, and also a tendency, which is to be deplored, for attitudes to polarize: tempers rise, mutual recriminations are exchanged, and the more reasonable middle ground tends to be ignored. Thus reactions to the Risinghill affair tended to treat Mr Duane either as a villain or as a saint. Because I do not believe that 'the child is always right', I shall probably be considered hopelessly reactionary in some quarters, and because, on the other hand, I cannot see value in a purely suppressive discipline, others will think me a starry-eyed academic remote from the harsh realities of the schools – though universities at the present time of student unrest are not exactly ivory towers. It is precisely because most of my professional life has been concerned with teachers of less able children – where realities are at their sternest – that my conclusions about useful and useless methods of dealing with childish misdemeanours may be of value. The Mrs Halls of the teaching profession are in a minority, certainly, but there are enough of them for remarks to be made with accuracy and conviction about the most hopeful ways of tackling the 'submerged tenth' of the disaffected. It was not by chance that she overcame what had previously been considered a hopelessly intractable problem; her story could have been paralleled by that of many other teachers who believe in something more than useless suppression.

The study of 'discipline', then, tends to run into blind alleys of sensationalism or sentimentalism, and to raise too many stock responses to be conducive to intellectual enlightenment. The study of morale can, I believe, be more productive; firstly, because it has been less trampled over, secondly, because it is less immediately emotive, and, thirdly and above all, because it provides a positive approach.

We can divide our topic into individual morale, group morale, and teacher morale. The first will be taken up in this chapter, the latter two in subsequent ones. One would naturally expect physically strong and well-coordinated children to have higher morale than the weak and puny, the quick and able than the slow and dull, the emotionally secure than the insecure, and so on, going in turn through the factors that have relevance in the development of personality. So no doubt it would be, if other things were equal, but in the complex developmental field frequently other things are *not* equal, and the suggested model is too simple. The work of Staines (1958) on the development of the self-picture, and Rogers's demonstration (1951) that an inappropriate and objectively false self-picture can be tenaciously clung to even when it is self-defeating and inhibits the individual from achievement that theoretically should be well within his powers, should warn us against taking too easy a view. We must avoid the trap of equating achievement, in any field, with morale, though in ordinary circumstances one would expect to find them reasonably highly correlated. Nor must we interpret morale in moralistic terms, so that a so-called 'good' character is thought to evince higher morale than a 'bad' one. A criminal who has in effect said 'Evil, be thou my good' may be quite successfully living up to his aspirations. It is rather in the sphere of the self-picture and its congruence or incongruence with the individual's values and ideals that clarification is to be found. If there is a great discrepancy between the individual's perception of himself and what he would like himself to be, his personal morale is likely to be low, irrespective of his talents, his environment, and his achievements. On the other hand if he is comfortable and satisfied with himself, his morale is high, however mediocre he may seem to the outside world. 'Self-satisfied' is not a term of praise in our society and is frequently used with a derogatory air, as much as to say 'He may be satisfied with himself, but his standards are low and his level of aspirations ought to be higher'. This reproach in a particular case may or may not be justified, but that is not the point: the point is the disapproval, which perhaps makes 'self-satisfied' an unsuitable expression to use. Taken literally, however, the individual who is reasonably 'satisfied with' himself has a steady centre from which he can grow, as distinct from the striving individual who is always trying to be something else. There is the further complication that the analysts will tell us that the self-satisfaction may be more apparent than real, a blind to cover up inner uncertainty, and this may well be so in certain circumstances, but it does not affect the main issue, which is how we are to define morale. Nor are we concerned with the ethical calculus, whether it is better to be 'Socrates dissatisfied or a fool satisfied'.

Morale, then, can be described in terms of the congruence between the individual's perception of himself and what he would wish himself to be. It can be high in certain fields and low in others, but complicated as it may be, a general pattern is traceable. Realistically it is affected by a multitude of factors that are present in the individual's objective situation – his family and social class, his physical and emotional history, his talents and disabilities, etc. –

and unrealistically, it is affected by a number of subjective appraisals through which his self-picture has been biased. The resulting strengths and weaknesses may be based on his natural talents and disabilities as a ground plan, but differ from them in significant respects – acquired likes and dislikes, interests, hoodoos.

It will be useful now to take some examples to test our argument so far.

John comes from a professional family and attends a minor public school. He is the youngest of three and is doing less well than his brothers did at school. He is learning to think of himself as a comparative failure at school, except in art in which he is gifted. In so far as his parents set high store by academic success, he realizes that he is disappointing them. On the other hand, his social position makes for confidence, and his attendance, even in an average capacity, at a school of some prestige presumably sheds some reflected glory on him. Or does it? Is he proud of his school, even though he dislikes it? Would his morale have been higher, or lower, if he had attended a less exacting establishment? Is this a case where great expectations, instead of acting as a spur to endeavour (as admittedly they sometimes do) have resulted in overpressure? Alternatively, is it all passing off him like water from a duck's back? He has not introjected his parents' academic ideals, and since he sees no particular value in academic success it could be argued that his average status at school does not pose any especial threat to him, for he will make his own values and goals elsewhere. Whichever interpretation one chooses, at least it is evident that his morale at present is lower than the optimum.

Jean is a student at a College of Education, conscientious and hardworking. She told her personal tutor that at school the main emphasis was on university entrance, and the majority who sought other careers felt themselves persistently devalued. Although she had entered college with good A-levels she showed little confidence. To her, learning was not something that was worth while in itself, but an endless gradient on which, no matter how well you did, there was always something higher and better ahead. She had made it a matter of conscience always to work, not because of the intrinsic interest of the subject matter, but because one 'ought' to try to reach perfection though it was constantly out of reach. It was an entirely new idea to her that perfectionism might be unhealthy, and that acceptance of less exalted ideals could make her less demanding of herself, with a corresponding improvement in morale. (The interesting thing is that her work didn't then fall off, but on the contrary improved – a point that I shall return to and develop, in a subsequent chapter.)

Readers may object that we seem to be reaching a point where traditional motivation is getting inverted. Is it not desirable for teachers to encourage children to work as well and as hard as they can? Of course it is, and I have already admitted that in other circumstances and with other children, the high expectations that were too much for John could be a spur to increased effort. The more interest that parents take in their children's progress, the more likely the children are to themselves consider school work important, and to respond accordingly. This is well known, and confirmed repeatedly in investigations, e.g. those into patterns of attitudes among the different social classes. But there is an optimum, after which interest shades over into anxiety, and once anxiety has been raised, in parents or children, it may have a boomerang effect. Furthermore, it is not simply 'encouragement' that is involved, but rather a subtle *dis*-couragement. Jean was not encouraged by the attitudes of her school towards the second-class citizens who were not going on to university, nor was John by the disparaging remarks that were made about him in school reports. It is understandable for teachers to feel that nothing but the best is good enough and that standards must be kept high and uncompromised, but the fact remains that these schools made much more systematic use of discouragement than they did of encouragement – drawing out from children the best of which they were capable. (It does not necessarily follow that teachers, at any level, who are constantly to be heard criticizing their scholars or students are those who have the highest standards themselves.)

Another interesting point is that both these examples were of adolescents of reasonably good ability and it is disquieting that their morale should be so low. Failure, we must remember, is relative, and what to some other children might have been considerable success, to them felt like failure. I turn now to consider two examples of children in whom the failure is not merely relative but undoubted.

Both of them were non-readers at the age of eleven, and I choose them because we are so often (and usually rightly) reminded of the wide-ranging importance of this key subject in schools. Keith came from a reasonably good home, Bill from the slums. Keith's parents were worried by his lack of progress, and so was he. Bill had simply written off school and teachers and was well on the way to acquiring an antisocial reputation. Both of them were difficult problems for their teachers, for in both cases the original intellectual difficulty had been overlaid by secondary, acquired (emotional) complications. Probably most teachers would prefer to help Keith, because at least he was 'willing to try', and his home was 'backing him', whereas Bill was constantly in trouble and unwilling to cooperate in learning. Yet, oddly enough, just because his rejection of reading was genuine, Bill's morale was likely to be less damaged by his failure to learn than was Keith's. From a teacher's point of view, he would be much more of a nuisance, but because he had, so to speak, split reading off from himself, *he* was not at all a failure – it was not a part of his image of himself. That is, provided the rejection is genuine, and not an assumed defence. There are many non-readers who defensively reject reading, but who are hurt by their failure – Keith, for example, might eventually reach a stage where he assumed a 'don't care' cloak – but it is going beyond the evidence to insist that this is true of *all* non-readers. Bill is more likely to be one of those who has maintained his self-image at the cost of becoming anti-school and so his personal morale is not lowered though his attitude to school is very hostile. This exemplifies the point made earlier, that we must not confuse morale with morality. Keith is much the more conventionally moral figure of the two, but it is Bill who has retained his morale, aided by those regrettable antisocial forays in the playground that his teachers so deplore, where he proves himself the master by his fists. This is *his* field of self-expression and this is the ground on which he has chosen (literally) to fight. We can say that he is learning an antisocial pattern, but we can not say that he is falling short of his own values, and so his morale is not affected.

The relation between low morale, then, and school failure is not a straightforward one, and while on the whole the more successful children exhibit higher morale, as one would expect, exceptions do occur at both ends of the spectrum. One of the most important tasks of schools, and one which by no means all schools perform satisfactorily, is to remain positive and encouraging to as many as possible of the children who attend them. This is not easy, and as schools become bigger and cater for an ever-widening range of abilities, it is likely to become harder rather than easier. John Holt (1964) in *How Children Fail* has described how schools dispense failure, and we need to think hard how this accusation can best be rebutted.

My last example in this section is of Gwen, a very ordinary child, neither as potentially able as John or Jean, nor as dramatically backward as Keith and Bill. What is her experience of school? Does she perceive it as negatively frustrating where all the things she can *not* do are paraded in front of her, or is it starred with moderate triumphs, so that in her inescapable ups and downs the positive preponderates? Since there are many Gwens to be found in every school, by definition, the answer to these questions is very important, since it will determine whether the general morale of her class and of her school is satisfactory, which will make a great deal of difference to the smooth running of the school.

I turn now to ask what criteria the teacher or lecturer can use to assess the state of morale of individual children or students in his care.

1. Is the pupil's usual attitude towards his work positive? Is he willing to have a go? When faced with new work, is his usual reaction 'I can't do it', almost before he knows what it is, or is he reasonably compliant and confident?

2. Does he appear to be learning at a rate commensurate with his presumed ability? The joker here, of course, is that prophecies tend to be self-fulfilling and a teacher who has already decided that John is not very clever is for that reason less likely to spot signs of unfulfilled promise (on the other hand, it *should* make him more ready to compliment John on his efforts, for if John genuinely is doing his best then there is no point in pressing him further).

3. Regular and punctual attendance is less reliable a sign of good morale than absences (especially frequent and spotty ones) and lateness are of poor morale. Where a reasonable level of conduct is maintained by sanctions, as in the case of punctuality, the mere maintenance of that standard tells one nothing as between indifference and good morale: it is only where real difficulty has been willingly overcome (as in the case of a boy with an awkward journey continuing to arrive on time during a transport strike) that one can say punctuality is evidence of good morale.

4. Much the same applies to school rules. Mere compliance with them is no evidence that morale is good, and good conduct of the sort that makes a child unobtrusive is perfectly compatible with indifference, dislike, and hostility towards the school regime. We are here concerned not with overt behaviour but with underlying attitudes, and the connection between them is not exact.

So the search for relatively objective tests of good morale in work, attendance, punctuality, conduct, is not very rewarding and we need to seek more elusive and subjective criteria.

5. Effort. At one end of the scale are passive individuals who go with the stream but put very little of themselves in their work. At the other end are those who appear febrile, over-anxious, over-driven. Whether the overdriving comes from others, parents and teachers, or from the individual's own excessively demanding superego, in either case the anxiety and tension preclude good morale. John and Jean are examples of these cases. Where effort

and enjoyment go together, there we are more likely to find good morale.

6. Freedom and gaiety are good indicants of morale. Freedom, not in the sense of absence of control or of doing what you like, but rather in the sense of doing things that you enjoy doing, and liking what you do. A happy child in a favourite lesson is not running wild, he is not destructive, nor is he passive. Unhappy children in detested lessons may well be all three – unless they are restrained by fear of the teacher's anger, but this puts the teacher in the ungrateful role of gaoler and turns discipline into a maintenance of sanctions. Granted that pupils will not always be in the fortunate position of liking what they do, and may sometimes have to do uncongenial tasks, their morale is good if on balance the positive predominates. When a child says (and means) 'I like school', he is not saying that he likes everything within it, but that enough of it is favourable for him to be willing up to a point to cooperate in the less attractive sections. So he learns to postpone satisfaction and to tolerate doing something not immediately attractive – unless there was this positive balance, there would be no incentive to overcome the things that he finds difficult and dull. Hence when morale is bad, a child cannot believe or trust that it will be worth while to cooperate – and so withdraws into passivity, or reacts with open rejection and troublemaking. The former attitude – of learning to postpone satisfaction – helps a child on the road to maturity, but the latter one if it persists is a block to development.

7. When we turn from schoolchildren to students, the position alters in that, in form at least, the students are free agents. They are over the age of compulsory attendance and have presumably taken themselves to college voluntarily, feeling that the game is worth the candle. Nevertheless, sanctions remain, of which the greatest is the need to gain a qualification finally, with the corresponding fear of failure. But if the fear of failure is the predominant motive overriding more positive motives such as interest in the work or desire to qualify, then morale cannot but be low. Irrespective of

I

whether or not the student actively rebels and joins in demonstra-
tions, if he feels no particular personal responsibility for his work,
but expects to wait until it has been set by somebody else and then
does it passively, he is acting as an automaton (even if a hardworking and well-behaved automaton) and is not really putting
himself into what he is doing. This was the case with Jean in our
example. To her, work was something which was 'set' by the
lecturers and 'done' by the students and while she was prepared to
cooperate most conscientiously and so counted as a good student
as well as an able one, she cannot be said to have high morale. In
one sense every student, since he has chosen to go to college, has
assumed a personal responsibility for his work unlike that of the
immature schoolchild, but in a more fundamental sense of acceptance the responsibility for learning may still be felt as being outside
the student and on the tutor or lecturer. I suggest that one distin-
guishing mark of good morale at the college or further-education
level is that the student not merely wants to pass, but wants to learn,
and is willing to put himself into his work. A number of students
at a party were asked in turn whether they were enjoying their
studies. It was the sort of occasion where a casual inquiry by a
stranger could easily and acceptably receive a flip reply, 'Awful!',
'Too much work', or gushingly 'Marvellous'. Instead, the visitor
was interested to notice that they all steadied down, and paused,
and seemed to think, so that their replies came from a greater depth
than the situation would normally call for. Their work really
meant something to them. This fundamental seriousness can go
along with, and be enhanced by, what I have earlier called gaiety
and enjoyment. It is a condition of involvement and does not
preclude lightness and laughter.

8. Above all, a situation of good morale is characterized by trust
and confidence. This is not merely a feeling that you can trust the
teacher to be fair all round, though this may be one of the necessary ingredients, without which a basic feeling of confidence cannot
be expected. (And many teachers do in fact fall down on this basic
fairness towards the unattractive, the troublesome, and the dull.)

It is not just a matter of leaving alone in a *laissez-faire* way: some-how a feeling of active acceptance has to be communicated. Given this feeling of acceptance, an individual is encouraged to show more of himself. He behaves more freely since he is less cautious and on guard. Paradoxically, it may be a good sign if a tense child begins to misbehave and allows himself to try out his confidence in his teacher. This does not mean that the misbehaviour itself is good, but it does mean that the teacher distinguishes between the unacceptable behaviour (which he does not condone) and the per-son, and makes it clear that the latter is still acceptable. Relation-ships cannot be legislated for, and the official standing of an individual as housemaster, counsellor, probation officer, or tutor in no way implies that he will be accepted, his advice sought, and his counsel taken. The wind bloweth where it listeth, and people go for help to those whom they naturally trust, irrespective of the official channels that have been dug. We should not deceive our-selves that the mere appointment of well-qualified and excellent counsellors will solve everything, because there is first the prior problem of how the counsellors are going to become known to the children. Since in fact the growing impersonality of schools is making it harder for teachers to be known as individuals to the children, and the children to the teachers, we have here an impor-tant cause of poorish morale, as the natural growth of relationships of trust and confidence between teachers and a particular child is rooted in shallower soil. 'We first raise a dust, and then complain we cannot see.'

It is vital for teachers to give the impression that they are on the child's side, irrespective of any little differences of opinion that there may be from time to time regarding undone work, broken rules, and unsatisfactory conduct – but, how can one 'give the impression'? Here, no sleight of hand will work, and there is no short cut by which that impression can be given short of actually *being* on the child's side. This is not within the voluntary control of the teacher (though, as I shall argue in the next chapter, there are ways in which one can *try* to put oneself into a more sympathetic viewpoint, but not expecting to achieve 100 per cent success) and so there will always be some children with whom a teacher fails. Someone else may succeed, and that is the main thing, that somewhere within the school there should be someone to whom each child can relate spontaneously and confidently, to take him from his isolation and improve his morale.

II Group Morale

Teachers frequently notice how much difference there can be between a group and its component members. Thus the individuals, taken separately, may be pleasant and ordinary but the group as a whole difficult to deal with; or more rarely it can happen that a group containing some quite difficult individuals may fit in well and function as a harmonious whole. Where the teacher is young, it may be suspected that his inexperience is a factor in the former, commoner, situation – it is not so much that the group is (inherently) difficult as that he finds them so. But inexperience apart, the phenomenon is sufficiently usual to be worth consideration. Without going so far as to posit a 'group mind' as some philosophers have done, the elusive but pervasive element sometimes called 'tone', sometimes 'atmosphere', cannot be left out of account. Visitors to a school quickly sense its atmosphere and usually agree closely in their descriptions of it, yet it is difficult to characterize in detail. One school may have a busy, purposeful atmosphere, a second may be pleasant but appear to be drifting, a third seem overcontrolled and so on. In the first part of the book I gave a number of case studies involving different atmospheres, and now we must try to analyse how group morale, good and bad, is built up.

Let us start with a small group, containing not more than six members, such as might be contained in the back right-hand corner of the classroom. We may hypothesize that they are not an entirely random sample: if self-selected they are likely to contain a greater than average number of children who are tall, or long-sighted, or uninterested in their work; if teacher-selected, they may be more than usually reliable and industrious. In either case, the natures and attributes of the individuals making up the group will be relevant. Secondly, we will need to observe the opportunities they get to form a composite entity, and this will depend on whether group work is usual, or rare, i.e. on the teacher's organization. Thirdly, whether the group continues to sit together when in other specialist rooms or to play together in breaks, i.e. is forming a coherent entity. Fourthly, whether it is being characterized as a group in references by teacher or children – 'that lot over there', 'Jimmy's gang', and the like. Fifthly, whether it considers *itself* as an entity – 'our lot', 'my friends', etc. A large number of detailed observations are made, which are then analysed into categories. (The method is that used in 'The Joint Fieldwork Exercise', where we saw how a number of trifling episodes can add up to form a pattern which can then be studied: a similar method is used by Gardner and Cass (1965). As it is time-consuming, detail will be omitted, and only the conclusions given here.) From observations of the interactions between teachers and the six children we find that Jimmy and Bob are often being reprimanded, Henry is ignored, Malcolm is a big nuisance to one teacher only but is no trouble elsewhere, and Ralph and Tim are averagely variable. Supplementing direct observation with sociometric material, we find that while Jimmy and Bob choose each other, and Henry chooses Jimmy, the others direct their choices elsewhere, outside the supposed gang. Evidently the commitment of Ralph, Malcolm, and Tim is less than had been thought and the gang less coherent. A check is made, and it is found to be Jimmy or Bob who talks about 'our lot' or 'my friends', bolstering up his personal morale by appeal to a group morale that as yet hardly exists. The situation may be different at the end of the year.

And so it goes on, a constant ebb and flow of individual and group fortunes. The less popular boys may band together – any port in a storm – irrespective of whether or not they would have preferred other more favoured friends, but they have to put up with what they can get. The rest of the class regard them without favour, taking their cue from the teachers, who have little time for them (it is astonishing how quickly children can pick up unspoken attitudes even when the teachers try, as they do not always do, to be scrupulously fair). An underprivileged group is in the making.

The low morale of this group comes from at least two sources. First, the individuals bring their low personal morale to it; second, they have no particular pride in the group as such, for membership of it carries little prestige, and they would prefer to sink their nonentities into a more glamorous corporate body, had they any choice. Jimmy gets a little boost from his supposed leadership, but, since his followers are unenthusiastic, he is a potential leader without any followers. 'And a good thing too!' say the teachers, thankful that Jimmy has little influence, and fearful that, if he had more, their maintenance of order would be more at risk.

But the existence of underprivileged subgroups is a threat to the stability of the whole class. It only needs one or two troublesome new boys for the balance of alliances to be affected in the class as a whole, and for Jimmy to become a more influential figure. The band-wagon effect may then operate in his favour, whereas previously public opinion tended to play him down. Social status fluctuates, and with it prestige and the pattern of morale in the class. (Similarly, there always have been individual disaffected students, the Jimmies of our colleges, but it is when the balance of power shifts that disaffection comes more into the open and is found to be more general than had been realized.) So teachers and lecturers cannot afford to be complacent that their under-privileged subgroups lack influence: this may not always be the case.

We have seen how the loose constellation round Jimmy has formed: we need to consider now how the subgroups themselves form different configurations within the class. Are they tightly organized, or fluid? Are there tensions and rivalries between gangs, or is there general amiability and good feeling so that loyalty to the larger group prevails over purely sectional interests? Are there many unattached, isolated individuals? Through socio-metry we have a technique for studying these questions, and the most common forms which social organization within a class takes can be charted. It can be demonstrated that one class is deeply split between warring groups, that another is, socially, so unorganized that it provides little security to individuals, and that a third has a stable hierarchy. But these differences do not just happen, they are caused. Some of the factors involved are outside the control of the teacher (e.g. the social history of the neighbourhood and the pos-sible existence of strong local street rivalries) but others are not, and some of the most interesting work in this field has been that which has sought to trace possible connections between the type of organization and discipline used by the teacher or leader and the social interactions of the children. Lewin and his followers, for instance, classified social climates as authoritarian, *laissez-faire*, or democratic, and correlated their outcomes in child behaviour; while Anderson and his co-workers conducted a series of studies into the classroom personalities of teachers, and their effects on the children. Marked differences were found, and all investigators are agreed that the type of leadership proffered by the teacher is an important determinant of the reactions of the children.

All this work has a direct bearing on our topic of morale, and with it in mind, we will now use the case studies of Part One and summarize the part played in the formation of group feeling by the leaders, class teachers, or headteachers as the case may be, on lines similar to those already used in 'The Joint Fieldwork Exercise'.

The head of Towne   is definite
gives a clear lead
knows what she wants
has high standards
is hardworking

Because of these qualities, her influence is likely to be strong. But is it an influence that makes for good general morale? Besides these qualities, she also

    shows limited sympathies
    doesn't keep balance between opposing claims
    neglects needs of majority
    deals with effects, doesn't look at causes.

    Mrs Hall

    is firm
    sets clear limits

This was probably true of many stern teachers too. But, in addition to these qualities, she

    has realistic expectations
    sets suitable work
    is technically able to help (e.g. with reading difficulties)

Above all, her *attitudes* are positive, she

    is on their side
    trusts them
    builds up their confidence
    empathizes with them
    is genuinely interested in them

She influences both the girls and the staff, though, as one would expect, her influence cannot be as great as that of the head.

    The head of Othertown

    shows all-round fairness
    has wide sympathies
    has positive attitudes
    enjoys teaching

The policies she inculcates and her staff adopts are markedly different from those of Towne and the result is a much happier community.

    Mr Smith

    is friendly and pleasant
    makes quick easy contacts

    But also

    is rather muddled

gives appearance of democracy,
but surface only

allows things to drift

tries to run with hare and hunt
with hounds

doesn't respect his staff

is not respected himself

This example shows how lack of respect for others alienates them and results in a chaotic *laissez-faire* atmosphere in which the low morale of the staff is likely to be reflected (though the example doesn't say so) in low morale among the children.

Mr Walker   sees everything negatively
staff reflects his pessimism
low standards of behaviour among
children
dull curriculum
slipshod organization
general unpunctuality and
indifference.

Mr Day   is friendly and pleasant
makes contacts easily

These qualities he shares with Mr Smith, but whereas they were Mr Smith's only assets, and not enough, Mr Day also

is firm

gives trust and responsibility

helps his staff

takes his share of extra work

gradually encourages higher
standards

doesn't rush or press

has clear priorities

enjoys his work

respects his staff

gains respect of staff and children
(not merely popularity).

Miss Read
is alert and observant
doesn't get embroiled in
  unnecessary unpleasantness
  (with vicar)
has sense of humour
puts herself in place of children
has sympathetic regard for Miss
  Clare
builds up children's confidence.

When we take all these together, it seems to me that a pattern begins to emerge. It is not a simple pattern and the last thing I want to do is to build up a list of 'good' qualities that are associated with 'good' morale – on the contrary, as we have seen with Mr Smith, good qualities may not be enough, or, as we have seen with the head of Towne, the leadership provided may be strong without resulting in high morale. But there is a certain similarity in basic outline, however different the environment and circumstances, to justify the claim that the quality of leadership provided exerts a marked influence on the cohesion and morale of the group. The essential qualities appear to be awareness and sensitivity to the needs of others, willingness to be fair all round, purposefulness and the absence of drift, respect for others, and not least enjoyment. (The latter may perhaps surprise those who, like Jean, feel that to be morally respectable it is necessary to be deadly serious. In fact laughter is an excellent morale-builder.)

The examples taken together also raise another point that needs to be explicitly brought out. It is usually easy and always a temptation to blame circumstances when things go wrong. Gaymount school, for instance, was set in a very difficult area, in which defeatism was understandable, and it would be very natural to explain the slack discipline and low academic standards in terms of poor neighbourhood, bad homes, and disturbed children. But that that cannot have been the *whole* story is shown by the change brought about by Mr Day. The homes and district and children were the same, and the teachers were substantially the same, but what had altered was the quality of leadership. Undoubtedly the environment was a more difficult one than that, say, of Miss Read's village, and I am not denying the importance of environmental factors, but simply concerned that these should not be used as a sort of rubber-stamp explanation accepting defeatism as inevitable. Another way of putting this is to adopt Batten's (1967) suggestion that a useful question to ask is, 'What could the worker have done differently?', though it would be going too far to suggest that that approach *always* results in enlightenment, for sometimes the worker has done all that could humanly have been expected, but things still go wrong, simply because the whole situation is so unfavourable. Nevertheless it is an excellent corrective to the other – and more usual – extreme, for it is so much easier to project the blame for the intractable situation outwards on to the circumstances, or the environment, or the children. 'A bad workman always blames his tools.' A middle position seems to be the soundest, in which we neither overstate the individual leader's responsibility for the whole situation, nor understate it in defeatism by claiming that nothing *can* be done since the unfavourable circumstances inevitably will be too strong. A more optimistic inference seems permissible from the effectiveness of Mr Day in improving morale, and also from the improvements brought about by Mrs Hall, even though she was circumscribed in what she could accomplish, going against the mainstream of school values and attitudes.

I conclude that a class-teacher largely determines the tone of his class, and a headteacher that of the school, though other factors outside their control are also contributory.

This conclusion implies that it is not enough to gather information about Jimmy, Tim, Ralph, and all the other children in the class, their personalities, histories, and backgrounds . . . *ad nauseam*, we also need to know about the teacher.

1. Is he fair? Does he give a reasonable chance to everybody? Unless he does, there will be differential resentments, and group morale in his class will be unstable.

2. Does he provide suitable work and activities to keep the children

occupied and to engage their interests? Boredom from work that is too simple and discouragement from work that is too hard are alike productive of discontent. (The present move towards mixing wide ranges of attainment in one class may increase the teacher's difficulties, for it is not easy to provide adequately for widely differing needs.)

3. Is he technically able to give the help that the children need? It is obvious that a teacher must know enough about his subject to be able to keep up with the oldest and brightest of them: hence specialization. It is less generally realized, but equally essential, for teachers to be able to help the children *at the point at which they find difficulty*. A lot of trouble in remedial departments in secondary schools is traceable to the teacher's technical inability to give the necessary help. Willing as he may be, he just does not know what to do.

4. But is he willing? We touch now on the vexed question of teachers' attitudes, the crux of the problem. It is natural for teachers to react favourably to eager, bright, and biddable children and to react less favourably to the disaffected, the dull, and the disobedient. The second reaction, however, though natural, is one which causes a chain reaction of difficulties. Teachers who are not interested in children who won't bring them credit, and who reject those who find it harder to learn, are in effect placing their subject above people, and in return they are likely to be resented. Children, however dull, sense quickly whether or not they are accepted, and react accordingly. The secret of a successful teacher is that he relates to children *as people* (not as competent or incompetent mathematicians, musicians, or whatever) and that he meets the children at the point at which they are at present, not at that where he thinks they ought to be. So he retains a positive and helpful attitude, not a negative and rejecting one.

We have seen that feelings of failure (which may be subjective and relative) are prominent in lowering personal morale, and that unsuccessful subgroups are usually among the disaffected, so that it is no surprise (as with Towne, as with Hargreaves's Lancashire school) to find that morale and amenability tend to diminish as one travels from the A to the B to the C ... streams. Before putting this forward as a general rule, however, we need to look at a test case, the morale of children in special schools for the educationally subnormal. We might expect to find it exceptionally low, but this is not so, and generally the morale of children in ESN schools is much better than that of similar children remaining in secondary modern schools, because (a) they have been removed from the atmosphere of failure and provided with an environment designed to help them, (b) their work is suitable and usually their teachers know how to help them, (c) in general the attitudes of teachers in special schools are more understanding and less unsuitably demanding than those of teachers in ordinary schools. It is common to find that children are happy and gain in confidence, though their personal morale can be lowered if they gather that attendance at a special school carries a stigma (this is the opposite of John's case, where he was unhappy at a school he gained kudos from attending). So the defeatism that so often prevails at the bottom end of the secondary school, both among children and staff, is not necessary and doubly regrettable. I have often thought of a remark made by a man who returned to his work with backward children in a secondary modern school after a year away 'How normal they are!' During this year he had seen genuinely exceptional children, and realized that his own pupils were basically normal, in spite of the loud staffroom complaints about them – and he concluded that the school was largely manufacturing its own problems by its overexacting attitudes.

Taken at its simplest level, 'I am at home here – I belong' is the remark of the individual who gains strength and confidence from his membership of a group. 'It seems strange that a boy who actually contributes so little to the group's functioning should derive as much feeling of group identity as he does: somehow he seems to borrow some of the group's morale. It helps him just to realize he is part of a group that can function even though, as an individual, he is not able to offer much.' (Loughmiller, 1965, p. 13). It is for teachers to build up this feeling of belonging and to minimize feelings of rejection, isolation, and unwantedness.

At this stage, a reader may say: 'I take the point about the importance of my own attitudes. But I don't naturally suffer fools gladly and if I don't accept them, I don't. How can I learn to become more accepting?' This is a very valid query, and not easy to meet. It can best be approached along some such lines as these: 'Suppose instead of going to college where you naturally specialized in your best subjects, you had found yourself imprisoned for three years with your worst.– doing a degree in mathematics for which you have a hoodoo, at a PE College when you are hopelessly non-athletic, at the Slade when you can't draw, how would you have liked it? How would you have reacted?' The ability to put oneself in the place of the failing or nonconformist child or student is most valuable in enlarging one's sympathies, and the question 'How would I like it myself?', simple as it may sound, is as useful a key as any to open up channels of communication between successful brisk no-nonsense teacher, and unhappy bewildered unsuccessful child.

When asked how they would react if . . ., a group of teachers will usually produce a range of replies covering the whole spectrum from active troublesomeness through discouragement to apathy and despair – and then immediately realize the point that this is exactly the behaviour they complain of in the children. In fact, the children are simply producing the normal reactions to frustrating situations. And what then becomes of the sedulously held notion that these are abnormalities which prove how *different* these children are? The barriers are down, when the teacher realizes that he is a man of like clay, and instead of holding himself aloof in fancied superiority, recognizes that the children's difficulties and their awkward and uncouth reactions could in less favoured circumstances have been his own.

We now need to try to clear our minds on the purposes and results of different forms of grouping within schools, because at the present time a lot of confusion exists as to the principles which should govern a head's choice of forms of organization. In effect, a head has to decide whether he wants to aim for as much homogeneity as possible, or settle for heterogeneity. In the past, it was taken for granted that homogeneity was desirable, so that when schools were large enough, children were divided into classes according to age and perhaps sex and then again according to scholastic performance. More recently, not only has streaming come under attack, but heads have experimented with forms of family grouping, so that children of different ages work in the same class, and with team teaching, so that lateral class divisions are less strong than they used to be and the classroom walls in some cases literally have ceased to exist. If the result of this change of educational climate is that children are thought of simply as children, without extraneous labels, all of whom have an equal right to an education that develops their individuality, it is to be welcomed; but if it results in thinking of them as interchangeable units each of whom has to be given identical treatment, the end is a denial of individual differences and a reactionary return to the old lockstep of the nineteenth century. It should be remembered that in the first instance children were separated into different classes in an attempt to cater more suitably for their differing educational needs, the younger from the older, the slower from the brighter. (Obviously this process cannot be carried through in every respect in which children differ nor would it be desirable, so if children are homogeneous with regard to one or two dimensions they are heterogeneous with regard to all the rest physically, emotionally, and socially, and homogeneity can never be an absolute end.) It was claimed, and has recently been denied, that it is easier for teachers to cater suitably for a restricted range of ages and/or abilities than for children of widely varying attainments. Whether this is indeed so is a matter of teaching technique and is not particularly relevant to us here, but let us grant for the sake of the argument that one original principle in the adoption of streamed types of organization was that it could conceivably make it easier for teachers to provide suitably for the slow and the full whose morale is most at risk. What is not in doubt is that this streaming, however well intentioned in the first place it may have been, did in fact lead to discriminatory differences of a most undesirable kind, which are highly relevant to our topic of morale. It was not merely that the C stream was felt to be different: it was also felt to be worse, morally and socially as well as scholastically. The humiliating status of the C stream has been spelt out in detail in books such as those by Hargreaves (1967), Farley (1960), and Partridge (1966), all of which paint a depressing though undoubtedly justified picture of attitudes and morale in far too many streamed schools. Get rid of streaming; treat all children alike; abolish these invidious differences – these are the natural reactions of reformers.

But unfortunately the matter goes deeper than this, and a superficial 'We don't want them to feel different' is no solution. A regime of examinations, academically taught subjects, and foreign languages may be perfectly suitable for many children – and still be unsuitable for others. There is a basic dishonesty of thought in the unwillingness abroad at present to face the facts that different children have different educational needs – or rather, to face it half-way as far as high-fliers are concerned, and to refuse to consider the obverse of the picture. Much of the so-called non-streaming is simply a denial that difficulties exist: by lumping all children together the problems are swept under the carpet. But to make problems less noticeable is not the same as solving them. In my book *The Slow Learner* I have previously argued that the need for special educational treatment is not confined to the special school, but should exist also in the ordinary schools in the form of *suitable* educational treatment, which admits a range of gradations and is based on an acceptance of the fact that within a normal population there are many variables – in short, the acceptance of individual differences rather than their denial.

We are thus left with a confrontation: If you try to make special arrangements for slow learners, undesirable discriminations arise, and these are very bad for morale; but if you leave the slower children unnoticed, they are not helped, and this can be just as bad – 'A child cannot be more cruelly segregated than to be placed in a room where his failures separate him from other children who are experiencing success' (NSSE, 1950, p. 24). Can this contradiction be circumvented?

I feel that the real and unnoticed root of the trouble is an attitudinal one, and as long as this is left undisturbed, organizational changes will not help, or will help only marginally. Teachers and many parents have accustomed themselves to equate school failure with moral failure, and frequently import an attitude of blame into their judgements, rather than try to be acceptant of slowness as a fact which is in itself morally neutral. By extrapolating educational success or failure into the realm of morality, the stakes have been raised unjustifiably. Can one really suppose that a teacher whose unfavourable attitudes have been inculcated over years in conditions like those described by Partridge will in an unstreamed class become a model of fairness?

But at this point a real difference does come in. Jimmy and his mates may not be receiving any more help in their *work* from a teacher who quite genuinely does not know how to set about helping them, but the fact that they constitute a small portion only of an otherwise well-behaved class makes all the difference in the world to the general discipline of the class. As it runs more smoothly than the 'sink' composed entirely of malcontents, the teacher is likely to be much happier and more relaxed, and so more optimistic in her view of her charges, even Jimmy, than is the teacher (probably young and inexperienced, to make it all the more unfair!) of a generalized 'sink'. That is, from the point of view of school discipline, things may run much more easily when the known troublemakers have been split up than when they are all congregated together. But morale is less likely than discipline to be favourably affected by external changes unless something is done to really help the children and remove the pervading feeling of failure and rejection. This brings us back to the technical aspects of teaching – is the teacher equipped to help at the point of failure?

Technical qualifications are a much more acceptable principle of homogeneity. It stands to reason that where elaborate equipment is provided, say for physically handicapped or deaf children, then for maximum profit the children should be in need of this provision, i.e. should be homogeneous in this respect (though in other respects they are heterogeneous). Similarly with sixth-form studies – highly qualified specialists cannot be wastefully used. Similarly too with teachers who have the imagination and the skill to remedy children's difficulties – it would be a pity to have a qualified teacher of the deaf working with an ordinary unstreamed class if next door there are slightly deaf children who would profit by his expertise, or to have the only infant-trained teacher on a secondary staff confined to a programme that does not make use of her special abilities when there are several non-readers scattered through the school who need help. Whether in this latter example the help is given by class streaming or on a group remedial basis, in either case the point is the same, that the teacher's skills and the needs of the children are matched as well as possible. Pure heterogeneity is no more attainable than pure homogeneity, nor is it any more desirable. A random ragbag or brantub can by no stretch of imagination be called a school. I conclude that homogeneity of (bad) behaviour is no principle for grouping together, but that homogeneity of educational need may be.

A final point while on this question of homogeneity needs to be made. It sometimes happens that one particular class is well catered for, and so evinces more positive morale than its lowly place in the school hierarchy would lead one to expect. Where this is so, its place as troublemaker in the school is frequently taken over by another just above it in the school status system. We had an example of this at Towne. When Mrs Hall had won over her girls in 3R, it was the girls of 3C who achieved the greatest notoriety. This fact should surely lead us to conclude that it is not the intractable nature of the individuals and groups concerned that renders a particular problem insoluble, but rather the continued shortage of teachers of calibre sufficient to contain the disaffected, help them where they need help, gain their trust and confidence, and so finally, painfully and slowly, reach a stage where the morale of the group can be raised to a pitch not merely where complaints cease, but where their positive contributions to the school as a whole can be appreciated.

> *Who sweeps a room, as for Thy laws*
> *Makes that and the action fine.*

The positive correlation so often found between low educational status and low group morale is not a law of human nature, but rather an example of human failure on the part of teachers, parents, and society.

It will be noticed that in this discussion of streaming I have deliberately avoided the usual angle from which the subject is discussed, that of social class. While agreeing that resentments and misunderstandings between the different social classes may be an important factor in the rejection of teacher or taught, I feel the ground has been sufficiently trampled over in this direction, and a further difficulty is that it raises strong prejudices and political overtones that obscure the basic educational problem. To me, this seems to be best phrased in terms of relative heterogeneity or homogeneity. If we decide that relative heterogeneity is preferable in some respects and homogeneity in others (a tame and unsensational conclusion when one thinks of all the impassioned ink that has been spilt over it!) we still are left with the problem how in either form of organization teachers' attitudes can become more helpful and accepting to the less successful children.

Nothing could be more dangerous than a search for panaceas, uncritically adopted, as non-streaming tends to be at the present time. We need to remember that, after all, sports teams and choirs seem to be able to operate on a homogeneity principle without raising cries of class discrimination! To give everyone a fair chance is not the same as treating them all as interchangeable units. It is ironic that the C stream, which on the face of it could be a reasonable attempt to educate children in accordance with their age, ability, and aptitude, should have ended in a morass of discriminatory attitudes – but it is the attitudes that should concern us most.

What are the reasons that make teaching slow children so unpopular?

1. The children cannot produce work of such a high standard. This depresses a subject-oriented teacher.

2. The children often behave badly.

3. The teacher realizes he does not know how to help them and this makes him feel his teaching has failed. He responds to the frustration they cause him with just the same gamut of reactions as they do to their own failure!

4. It is likely that the head has similar attitudes, and the value-system of the school and its hierarchy of promotion reflects them.

5. The teacher feels himself undervalued. Again, he is in the position of the children, and, again, his range of possible reactions is analogous to theirs.

The vicious circle is complete. The morale of the unwilling teacher is soon no higher than that of his pupils. He gets out if he can, to something more rewarding, and if he cannot is confirmed in his unsuccessful self-picture.

It is evident that we must next examine the morale of teachers.

III The Morale of Teachers

Logically, this is a special case of group morale, for in some ways the relationship of head and staff is analogous to that of teacher with class, but I am treating it separately because of its importance. Points already covered that apply include the head's need to give a clear lead, to be fair and consistent, to respect his staff, and above all to be positive and helpful rather than merely negative and critical.

Here are some of the factors that appear to be relevant in considering the state of teacher morale at any one time. I will begin by mentioning the more general factors, and continue in greater detail with those that are more germane to my theme.

1. Public esteem – how far teachers, as teachers, are respected by the general public.

2. Salaries. To some extent repeated salary claims are not only for more money, but also for a higher place in public esteem. Money is regarded as a yardstick of this, and where salaries are low, they are resented not only in themselves, but as a sign that the general status of teachers is not as high as teachers would wish.

3. The way in which the total amount available (high or low) is allocated. Graded posts are a fruitful source of controversy, arguments, and jealousies. There is evidence that they increase mobility

between schools beyond the optimum, as teachers move from school to school in search of higher allowances, and staffing instability results.

4. Wastage. The very high figures that are sometimes quoted in press articles may overstate the position, since many of the women who leave to raise a family will return to teaching later, and movement to other posts in the educational service (e.g. to administration) is included as wastage, but when these points are allowed for the number of those who start teaching and then give it up can be regarded as an index of job dissatisfaction.

5. Staff turnover. Schools in some districts are notoriously more difficult to staff than others, but even in 'good' districts some schools have a constantly changing staff.

6. Staff absences. Happy people tend to be less often ill than unhappy ones, and when they are ill, are more likely to make the effort to turn up at work notwithstanding. If very large schools, for example, were found to have higher absence rates than smaller ones, it could be an important index of teacher morale there.

7. Early retirement. The number of those who retire as early as they can and sooner than they must is a sign of morale.

8. The growing complexity of schools means a greatly increased burden of administration. It has been said, 'If you double the size of a school, you quadruple the administration.' The timetable becomes immensely complicated and the cumbersome structure tends to be unwieldy and not easily adaptable to meet necessary changes.

9. As schools become more impersonal, it becomes less easy for teachers to see the effectiveness of their work. When it is harder to see who is responsible for what, the less conscientious can get by, the more conscientious resent this, and the able become discouraged.

10. With earlier maturity on average, resentment at pupillage grows, and children become more difficult to control, so that more time is spent by the teachers in settling disturbances, with all-round dissatisfaction among both teachers and children.

11. Conditions in schools have improved considerably over the last twenty years. Buildings are better, much more money is spent on equipment, and more technical help is available to look after it. Teachers work in more pleasant physical surroundings than they used to do.

12. Many more facilities are available for teachers to improve their qualifications. Leave of absence for degrees, secondment to take in-service courses, the recent development of Teachers' Centres – all mean a readier access to ideas, and more cross-fertilization as a result.

If one attempts to build up a balance sheet from this complex picture, it is evident that contrary trends are involved. The direction of change in some instances appears to be favourable, in others unfavourable. Thus, for instance, better buildings have to be balanced against rather less satisfying work, the outer against the inner. It is easy to see the nice new building and the good facilities, but it is less easy to see the imponderables which nevertheless have strong influence. I would sum these up under the word 'pressure'. This is a word which one is constantly hearing now, and heard much less often ten years ago: I believe it to be very significant. Even factors that at first glance one would take to be wholly favourable, such as the improved qualifications of teachers, are expressed in some such form as 'the pressure on teachers to improve their qualifications', i.e. subjectively it is *felt* as pressure. Constantly rising standards, however desirable in themselves, may have a backwash of insecurity, and if the predominant motivation is less the inherent interest of the proposed course of study than a competitive desire to keep up with the well-qualified Joneses, its overall effect may be to increase uncertainty and lower morale. In effect, the teacher who feels that his personal qualities and teaching record are of little account is to that extent devalued. ('The Office wants Results quickly' is also relevant in this connection.) To what extent *have* the pressures on teachers increased? Newer forms of examining, such as the CSE, which increase the participation of teachers, are to be welcomed, but they do mean more work for those serving as examiners and on panels; more interchange at Teachers' Centres, again to be welcomed, means more meetings and more calls on teachers' time; out-of-school activities have greatly increased. These examples are taken from secondary schools, but corresponding examples could be found in primary schools, with a call for new subjects such as languages, or the development of new methods in mathematics or science. These are positive changes, containing much that is attractive and interesting, and likely to be met in a positive spirit, but other sources of increased pressure, such as more frequent staff changes, less good relationships with the children, and the increasing claims of society on the schools, can less easily be welcomed. To take one simple example – in a small community there is no difficulty in the teacher knowing parents and neighbourhood as well as the children (he does that anyway), but in a large city the effort consciously to communicate with, much less to know intimately, the children's family background can be considerable – and is experienced as a *demand*, and hence as pressure, on the teachers rather than, as in the small community, as something acquired without conscious effort. Children who are not known (as individuals) are not well taught, but knowing children is more than just knowing their names, as those who teach in very large schools may sometimes very understandably be tempted to forget. I am impressed by the efforts made by good teachers in large schools to get to know the children well, but the point is that it *is* an effort and does not come naturally but has to be planned. The essence of teaching and its chief satisfactions (the contact of minds) may be sacrificed in the cause of increased efficiency, only to reveal that the increased efficiency is elusive, for overpressure and reduced satisfaction and morale exact their own penalty.

From these rather general considerations, I turn now to the individual school where the headmaster is face to face with his staff. Face to face? Well, perhaps not, because the same impersonality that we have observed in the contacts of teacher and children may also make the head a remote figure. A large school is in effect a combination of constellations intricately geared together, and much of the responsibility of the head for the welfare and encouragement of his staff is delegated, formally or by default, to the heads of departments and other senior figures who assume many of the pastoral functions with staff and children that would have been the head's in a smaller establishment. Even so, he retains the ultimate responsibility, and since the policies stem from him, in the last resort it is his values that are likely to count, and to be relayed perhaps in a diffused form, perhaps with some contradictions, by his intermediaries. Sometimes the centipede may seem to be moving in several directions at once! and the message of kindness and interest as received by one young teacher in one department with consequent effects on her developing morale may be very different from the message received by another young teacher in another department, with different consequences. In an earlier case-study we saw the disintegrative effect of weak and biased leadership on staff morale, not only at the level of the oligarchy, but also in spreading bloody-mindedness among junior members of staff. Even granted that Mr Smith had given a clear lead, there is no guarantee that it would have come through clearly when diffused through several intermediaries, so his task was doubly difficult when compared with that say of Mr Day or Miss Read. Mr Day, incidentally, was no superman, and the task that he faced, though difficult, did not call for superhuman powers for its solution. We cannot legislate on the assumption that an unlimited supply of supermen will be available, and while exceptional people may carry through the most difficult assignments successfully it is unwise to generalize from their success for that very reason. I believe it to be an important cause of poor morale among teachers at the present day that many of their leaders are being strained beyond their natural limits; and, being unable to carry the demanding responsibilities they are given, they not only break up themselves but spread demoralization among those with whom they work. It is the easiest thing in the world to be busy (as Parkinson's Law has it, work tends to occupy the time available for its performance) but not so easy to be *effectively* busy, because this involves the selection of priorities. Heads who cannot delegate are not only causing bottle-necks but also demonstrating their lack of trust in their subordinates to do the job properly, to the consequent detriment of morale. What is important in a head is rather the opposite quality, the ability to set teachers free so that they are willing to go ahead on their own, confidently, but within the limits of a generally agreed policy that has been fully discussed with them, that they have had a hand in shaping, and that they can comprehend. This democratic approach is valuable for several reasons: (1) it underwrites and assumes the competence of the members of staff, and therefore is confidence-building; (2) by calling for contributions from all, as wide as possible an array of points of view is invoked; (3) differences of opinion, and misunderstandings, are ironed out beforehand. A façade of democracy is seen in staff meetings that have no real power and do not discuss important issues; these are worse than useless, and serve only to decrease, rather than increase, morale. People are willing to give their time when they can see that it is being used to good purpose, but they resent, and see through, window-dressing. One of the most difficult problems we now face is to work out effective channels of communication within the large school – too much paperwork will clog these channels, and only result in a waste of effort since long screeds are usually not read, and yet everybody needs to know clearly what is going on, and to be informed in essentials even if not in all the details. Wasteful overlapping and duplication of effort is destructive of morale, and leads only to demarcation disputes as to who should do what; once quarrels arise on this score we can say good-bye to solving our problem of communication, for the members will be more occupied in forwarding their own competing claims than in trying to understand the point of view of others, and so counsel will be darkened and chaos supervene.

Finally, whatever the state of public esteem, whatever the helpfulness or unhelpfulness of the particular school in which he is placed, in the last resort the teacher's morale will depend on his own values and attitudes. If he perceives his work as interesting and intrinsically worth while he is more likely to withstand lack of social prestige and an indifferent common-room (though obviously these will do nothing to help him) and through his own belief in his work and his self-respect, earn also the respect of the children he teaches.

So we come back to teachers' perceptions of themselves and their actual work with the children. Do they think of it as socially valuable, absorbing, satisfying to the mind and heart? I propose to answer this key question with particular reference to teachers of slow children. I choose this group, firstly, because they are the ones that I have been privileged to work with for twenty years and so know most about, and, secondly, because of all teachers they are the ones who are nearest to the rub and therefore their reactions are peculiarly valuable. If it can be demonstrated that the depressing vicious circle with which the previous chapter ended can be broken, the message of optimism is likely to be more generally relevant to more teachers than if, say, it was demonstrated that certain teachers at Eton or at Roedean evinced high morale. Thirdly, it ties up with what was said in the previous chapter about the morale of slow children being most at risk.

I will begin first with teachers who work in special ESN schools, where the position is easier to characterize than in the confused situation at the bottom of the ordinary schools. Fifteen years ago, I wrote in *The Slow Learner* that teachers in ESN schools tended to be either very bad or very good, with few 'middling' teachers. This was because at that time some ESN schools were difficult to staff and so very weak members had to be retained, having sunk through the hierarchy and at last come to rest there; but alongside them were to be found unusually able, imaginative, and skilful teachers who had reached the special school by a positive process of self-selection, not by a process of drift. These were teachers who had deliberately chosen to follow their values and as was to be expected their morale was high, as that of the former group was low.

In the intervening years ESN schools have improved their public image considerably, partly as a result of the work of good teachers, partly through increased public interest, and partly through attractive new buildings. Competition for posts in them is keener, and the dead-end placements are fewer. Teaching in ESN schools is now not merely socially respectable, but carries a certain kudos. Thus other teachers will often say admiringly, 'How patient you must be', even if they have no desire themselves to show that patience, and they will less often say, 'You must be mad to think of going there'. It has been said that just as infant and nursery schools provided the growing-points where the most interesting work was going on between the wars, so the special schools have provided the growing-points in education since 1945. The good teacher in ESN schools was never in doubt about the value of his work and its call on mental and moral as well as physical stamina, but, whereas earlier he was going against the stream, the tide has now turned and he will find his personal convictions echoed and reinforced by the weight of public approval. There is general recognition not only of the social value of the work of ESN schools, but also of their part in forwarding educational advance by experiments in teaching methods, work experience, etc. In many areas ESN schools are in the van of educational progress. While the children still need sympathy (and this is now more often shown than scorn) the teachers are looked on with respect – if still from a distance. The result of this favourable social regard is that teachers no longer need such tough pioneering qualities in order to maintain the high morale that many teachers in special schools have always had. It is also true that the conditions in which these teachers work – a small community, close relations with children and colleagues, immediate feedback – are increasingly rare in English education today, and are themselves intimately related to the maintenance of pleasure and pride in one's work.

I would say unhesitatingly that the morale of teachers in ESN schools, as a group, is high – probably higher than that of most other groups. This can be tested by the objective criteria I suggested at the beginning of this chapter – attendance, low wastage, low turnover, etc. I said earlier of the children in ESN schools, that, happy as they usually are there, their morale is ambivalent since they are aware that society looks down on their incapacity, but this ambivalence does not apply to the teachers, who are now usually supported by society.

The paradoxes of society's attitudes to failing children – rejection in the ordinary school, sympathy to those officially designated 'handicapped' in the special school – come out again towards the teachers. The slightly unwilling respect now shown to special-school teachers is not usually extended to teachers of slow children in ordinary schools. These frequently have the worst of both worlds in that they are thrown up against the competitive value-system of the ordinary school without the safety-valve of being 'special', and distant. Since their children are officially 'ordinary', they may be expected to conform to an unimaginative regime without any allowances being made, and there is no kudos going for teaching in such conditions. On the contrary it is frequently inferred, and sometimes stated, that only unsuccessful teachers will be found with unsuccessful children. The skill needed to teach backward children, having been conceded as far as special schools are concerned, is not extended to the lower echelons of the ordinary school by public opinion (which includes other teachers, parents, and the general body of children). All this in a setting where feedback is delayed, relationships are of necessity more impersonal, and pace and pressures are greatly increased, means that, as compared with the special-school teacher, the teacher of backward children in the ordinary school has a formidably unpromising task – unpromising alike as regards public opinion, the mechanics of the situation, and the sheer size of the problem. So it is not to be wondered at if morale is frequently low.

In some respects, the situation in the ordinary schools today is comparable to that in special schools fifteen years ago – teachers of the less able children tend to be either bad or good. Alongside those who have drifted into work with the so-called remedial classes not through any particular desire or skill, but simply because the large number of unfilled vacancies there is the last refuge of the least aspiring or the first post of the inexperienced, are to be found a number of excellent and skilful remedial teachers. The former group bear out the scepticisms of public opinion, the latter group refute them. But, because numbers are so much greater, the highly motivated group are much more in the minority than they were in the earlier ESN situation and it is therefore doubtful whether they will succeed in bringing about a revolution in public attitudes compared with that of which the special school was the beneficiary. The lump to be leavened is so much bigger.

But that the convinced minority exists at all is surprising and heartening. In one comprehensive school the head of the remedial department working over a period of ten years gained the respect of her colleagues and aroused their interest in the children under her care so that they became more ready to consider the children positively as a challenge to their teaching skill than negatively as a challenge to their powers of suppression. The children became more confident as their bridgehead of security widened to include not only Mrs X but several of her specialist colleagues and they became less of a disciplinary problem. Mrs X was helped in staff estimation by having a good specialist subject herself which she taught successfully at examination level, and by having the backing of a fair-minded headmaster, and on any reckoning she was a most able teacher, well able to give the lie to crude stereotypes of the 'backward teacher' variety. Her morale was strong enough to maintain her over a long stretch of time, not a transitory flash. Quite simply, she enjoyed teaching, at all levels. In a composite portrait of a number of such teachers whom I have known, similar traits would constantly recur. 'He likes his work', 'she does a real professional job', 'complete devotion to the children's interests', 'ability to put himself into the child's place', and the like.

In this overall picture, it will help our understanding if we distinguish between attitudes on the one hand and know-how on the other, though obviously, the two are interconnected. Mrs X did not have favourable attitudes out of the blue – she had them partly because her basic technical teaching skills were sound enough to enable her to offer help to the children at the points where they were failing. I am convinced that one of the reasons why many teachers do not want to teach slow children is that they genuinely do not know what to do with them. It is easier to take refuge in half-understood but impressive-sounding words which can be used as diagnostic labels and often as reasons why nothing can be done than it is to settle down and really study children as children and find out how they can be helped. Equally, it works the other way, for a teacher whose attitudes are unfavourable is unlikely to take the trouble to learn new teaching techniques.

I read a most interesting unpublished account from a teacher in a very unsympathetic secondary school whose interest in the plight of the tail-enders was stirred. An art specialist himself, he was well aware that he had no idea what to do in basic subjects, but he dragged himself up by his own boot straps, and sought and experimented and inquired and tried out again and learnt from his mistakes until finally he developed his own basic teaching skill – so it can be done. This unpretentious account is worth a dozen more elaborate but more distant theses.

The conclusion one must reach from all this is that when teachers want to help the slower children, and know how to, it is a very satisfying job, and their morale is high – as long as they do not get discouraged by having to row against the stream and as long as they get reasonable recognition (which they do not always do) from colleagues and heads.

The last topic to be discussed in this chapter will be the effect on teacher-morale of what is sometimes called the explosion of knowledge. In all subjects and at all stages of education the sheer factual content has increased sharply, syllabuses quickly get out of date, new material is crowding in as older material becomes obsolescent, and techniques become ever more elaborate. At each stage of education more is demanded of pupils with even greater expectations from the succeeding stage. Teachers are at the point of mediation between the increasing mass of material and the pupils or students for whom it has to be winnowed, selected, and processed. It becomes even harder for teachers, never mind children, to see the wood for the trees. One thing can be said with certainty, that if the teacher or tutor is muddled, the children or students will also be – more so. The impression is gained that it is becoming more difficult for teachers at all levels to keep intellectually abreast of the factual content of the subjects they have to teach, let alone extract meaning and pattern from them. And it is this latter which is the essential task of any teacher worthy of the name – to be able not merely to transmit an undifferentiated mass of undigested material to his pupils or students, but to be selective and clear. If he hasn't digested the material himself, then still less will his pupils. Simplicity, clarity, and sincerity are the hallmarks of good teaching, but there is danger of their replacement by turgid and half-understood complexities. The disengagement of principles from a mass of confusing detail calls for understanding: without it, the last state may well be worse than the first, and allow the uncomprehending individual to overlook large-scale errors of far greater account than the relatively trifling errors of detail that his first simpler explanation held – by straining at gnats, we may end up by swallowing camels. So the teacher's first duty is to simplify complexities according to the understanding of his pupils, not to pour in more and ever more. A student is not helped by being told to read six books, in none of which the underlying structure is clear, and which simply repeat six times over the same elaborate and confused conglomeration of data: this only means chaos which he tries to cover up by using impressive-sounding polysyllables. He feels he has worked very hard, but he has not furthered his understanding. In my own field I have noted that teachers are hindered rather than helped by being exposed to a number of overelaborate ideas about backwardness which get in the way of their ability to make a simple and straightforward contact with their pupils. Modish claptrap abounds, and teachers feel they *have* to keep up to date. We may not yet have reached the advertiser's paradise where 'it's new' represents the ultimate recommendation, but we are working that way.

In case this sounds like a call for lowering standards, I would reply that no standards have ever been raised by abandoning understanding. The additional knowledge is to be welcomed for its own sake, but not worshipped: it has to be woven into an understood pattern, but not slapped on from outside. The extent to which a teacher can internalize and make his own the diverse and warring complexities that surround him will determine his freedom of mental manœuvre and to a large extent his morale. As an example – there is much unreal knowledge bandied about in educational courses, unreal because it is not taken sincerely, not internalized, and not applied. The proof of the pudding is in the eating and only through application can wisdom come. To help his morale, a teacher needs not only knowledge, but also the wisdom that comes from a long perspective, thorough understanding, and the ability to put precepts into practice – and nobody, as far as I am aware, has yet been talking of an explosion of wisdom. Now that would be worth having!

IV Productiveness and Social Learning

As one reads through the case studies in Part One, one becomes aware of a difference in tone between some of the later ones and, say, the Joint Fieldwork Exercise. It is not just a matter of duration, though obviously the length of time a group remains together will be a relevant factor in considering the contacts that develop: another dimension is involved. The speaker in 'In Retrospect' was talking at a level of experience that could not have been reached in the short field course. This was not only nor even mainly because of the time element; however long the field course had lasted it showed no promise of being other than a superficial group experience, inhibiting rather than encouraging deeper contacts. Some group relationships begin, and remain, superficial, while others begin, as they must, superficially, but develop strengths and depths that can have great influence on social learning, and hence on the work and productiveness of members of the group. It is presumably the desire of all teachers and lecturers that the education they provide shall be meaningful, or, in the current language of student protest, 'relevant'; but since one of the recurrent cries is a complaint that what students are offered is irrelevant to their real concerns, it is not a desire that is easily achieved. We need, first, to make a distinction between depth and complexity, for the word 'depth' is often used very loosely, and many teachers and lecturers unthinkingly take for granted that a mass of complex detail is working in depth, which it is not. There is also a difference between genuine difficulty (of ideas) and pseudo-difficulty (of obscure and pretentious language). Again, work that is intellectually difficult is not necessarily at a deep level, and one of the drawbacks in the explosion of knowledge mentioned at the end of the last chapter is that when data are habitually treated 'out of the top of the head' there may be no connection made with the rest of the person's life, as in the case of a psychology lecturer who does not apply any of his theoretical knowledge to his actual dealings with his students. As it becomes harder to see the wood for the trees, E. M. Forster's plea of 'Only connect' becomes more than ever important – and none the worse because it is expressed simply and straightforwardly.

Let us assume that a lecturer wishes to encourage significant learnings in his group. In what ways may he go about it? First, he may plunge straight in and go as deep as he can. A visiting lecturer, say in psychology, with a strange group of students may be tempted to be as sensational as possible, in hopes of 'presenting a challenge', 'waking them up', 'dispelling apathy', and the like. He stakes everything on what he calls getting a lively response – meaning by 'lively' as much excited argument as possible. He insists on being provocative and trailing his coat emotively. Sometimes he does not even believe himself in the case he is making, sometimes he is dazzled by his own rhetoric, but in either case he prides himself on raising fundamental issues and digging round (if not bulldozing) at the foundations of personality. He is dealing with deep and important issues – anxiety, sex, aggression – but is he dealing with them in depth? I would very much doubt it. Let us look more closely at the reactions of the students. The quality of their response is largely modelled on the quality of his stimulus, and as it was superficial (though dealing with serious issues) and sensational, so their response is naïve – anger, irritation, argument (of the sort that raises more heat than illumination). He has stirred up a lot of deep feelings, but he has also muddied them. Let us suppose he has been talking of the place of anxiety in learning. Much of what he says is true, but he had presented it in a negative way that releases more anxiety, which has to be noisily denied and pushed aside. Furthermore, we may question the contemptuous attitude to students implied in his hopes of waking them up. He *expects* them to be apathetic, sunk in ignorant sloth, until he goes along like a magician to unlock Pandora's box. Who is he, to presume to interpret to strangers their deeper feeling, and to arrogate to himself the right to crash in on their privacy? A little interpreting of his own role might be in order, but this is one step that is never taken, one veil that is never drawn aside. Why this coyness? Surely, what is sauce for the goose is sauce for the gander, and we need to look with very beady and irreverent eyes on the claims to instruct students of those who are themselves so insensitive as to be unaware of their crashing *bêtises* – or if they are not unaware, take pleasure in them, which is rather worse. I see no merit in the Angry Young Man approach, and feel no surprise that those who work in this way consistently report rivalry, strife, and tension to mark the intergroup relationships of their students. What else would you expect? But the fact that these are the results they achieve does not prove that these are the *only* results that *could* be achieved.*

A better direct approach, because more thoughtful and sincere, can be our second example. In this the lecturer, say, is relating delinquency to family tensions and disharmonies. Much of what he says can be deeply disturbing to any audience because it literally strikes home, and a group which felt that it was going to have a safely distanced talk about delinquency finds instead that much is relevant to the members' own lives and experience. The lecturer's manner evokes a positive response (instead of a negatively angry one as in the previous example) and because he is sincere, they respond to him with sincerity. They are quiet, but they *are* listening (any lecturer who doesn't know whether his class is awake or not unless they are angrily muttering cannot use his eyes), and

* For a fuller treatment of this, see my article 'Against Interpretation' (Cleugh, 1968).

considering, and relating what he says to what they know, both from books and also, very important, from personal experience. Some appear more uncomfortable than others outwardly, but this can be misleading and a blank face can cover deep concern, for instance in a student who himself comes from a broken home. My point is that striving for relevance and depth can cut both ways: while it is far preferable to a distantly theoretical talk on delinquency that externalizes it and pushes it away on to a distant 'them' who have nothing to do with 'us' and so can be treated as 'cases', it nevertheless raises its own problems, of which the chief is management of the anxiety it arouses. A sensitive lecturer will not wish to go too far, but if he is a relative stranger to his audience and does not know their individual circumstances, how is he to know what is too far? Even well done, the direct method of achieving depth by simply going to the deep end and pushing people in can have drawbacks.

In contrast to both these direct methods is an indirect one. Much slower and more time-consuming, it relies on the fact that group relationships need time to grow, and claims that a more lasting development in depth can be achieved by a quieter, less sensational approach which works from within rather than from without. In effect, the group rather than the lecturer dictates the pace of confrontation with deeply relevant issues. Individuals within the group have different needs, and some may be readier than others to consider problems at a significant level.

We will take as an example the management of anxiety concerned with the course of study pursued by the students. We can readily agree that some discussion of the students' own worries would be more relevant than an abstractly presented Psychology of Anxiety well larded with reading lists and a number of important names, which becomes just one more chore to be undertaken to add to the load. If it is done directly, though, by *telling* the students they are anxious, or if they're not, they ought to be (as in the first method of approach), great difficulties of timing arise. Students want to feel they are getting on (with the syllabus) and resent the dragging in of personal issues just about as much as they

resent being chained to the syllabus when their own concerns pre-
occupy them: you just can't win! Whatever the time you choose
it is bound to be wrong for some. Does this then mean that an
approach in the group is bound to be a failure, and that individual
chats with worried students is the only way? I do not think so:
obviously there is a place for individual approaches, but in addition there *can* be a valid place for group ventilation of ticklish
matters. The key is that it comes from a student or students; it is
not imposed on them by a lecturer.

The sequence of events may be something like this:

1st stage. Everything in the garden is lovely.

2nd stage. Gradually it ceases to be so lovely, but this won't be
admitted.

3rd stage. A student or students raises worrying matters such as fear
of failure. The others, still at the first or second stage, are not
ready for it to be openly discussed and block it off. *Nothing happens,*
and this is the crucial point where the oblique, non-directive
method differs from the earlier lecturer-centred approaches,
where the lecturer still persisted against the grain of student unwillingness. (Irrational as the opposition was to the discussion of
something they needed to have brought out into the open, for that
very reason it was unwise to persist.)

4th stage. The issue comes up again, and the discussants are numeri-
cally stronger. Somewhere along the line individuals are working
out their relations to other members of the group, almost as if they
were unconsciously deciding which ones they could trust and
which not – and also deciding whether their tutor could be trusted.
If he is perceived as uncomprehending or untrustworthy, student
anxieties will not be raised in front of him in the group. Having
been shut out he will not be able to help them *as a group*, though he
could (unless hopelessly uncomprehending) still be of use to individuals. The disquiet will persist, and will be discussed among
coteries, who will be able to help each other to a certain extent,
though not as much as could a senior person outside the group.

Let us suppose that they *are* able to speak freely in the presence of their tutor. The process continues.

5th stage. Students who hear others openly admitting that aspects of their work worry them begin to admit to themselves what they have previously refused to contemplate – that they too share these worries. (Contrast this with the noisy denial and pushing aside of the first example.) They may or may not join in openly as yet, but feel relieved that they are not the only ones. They look round the group and realize that it is always the one sitting next to them who seems so knowledgeable. A little insight comes at a time, and as it were incidentally. The tutorial group proceeds with most of its time and attention directed outwards, on to the syllabus, but with occasional glancing reflections inward. The pace of insight is unhurried, not forced, as when a whole lecture is given to 'Student Worries', however well and sympathetically done.

6th stage. The knowledgeable neighbour lets down his defences and admits his own concern! On the face of it that should increase the anxiety of other students, for if *he* can't do it, how much less can they? But, oddly, it seems much more comfortable all round, and fellow-feeling begins to emerge, as defensiveness decreases. It becomes easier to speak honestly and with less regard for effect and 'what will others think of me?' The group is now more realistic and less starry-eyed, but the worries openly agreed on have somehow become less menacing. They are still there, but can be coped with.

7th stage. Defensiveness continues to diminish all round. If it is not necessary to pretend one is something one isn't, then what one *is* can be allowed to emerge. People behave more comfortably, almost as if they were at home. A generally tolerant and acceptant atmosphere is engendered, and the unconscious feeling of rivalry of the early days, when it was almost as if each had to prove himself before a hostile throng, tends to sink into the background. Instead, it is replaced by a greater readiness to take what others say at its face value, to consider it, to test it, and perhaps accept it, rather than to shut one's ears against anything that is new because it might be too great a threat. So learning begins. Much of the work that is produced in this way by others is worthy of high respect, and a stage is reached where a happy group can be seen to be almost willing its members in turn to do well. Just as an unhappy group, torn by factions and jealousies, can lead to under-functioning because it is too dangerous to shine because it would lead to backbiting, so a happy group can encourage its members to perform to their utmost, perhaps beyond any previous expectation. A helpful circle is in process: the group encourages the individual, and the individual, supported and cushioned by the group, doesn't want to do anything slipshod that would lose him respect.

8th stage. As anxiety sinks into the background, positive feelings of self-worth are more in evidence. The students know they are working hard, but from a solid basis and not from a feeling of pressure. Learning becomes freer, gayer, more of a quest than a cattle-drive, and the element of creative open-endedness leads on further. A great increase in productiveness is accompanied by high morale, trust in the group, and confidence (as described in 'In Retrospect'). Individuals will then be heard to say, 'How nice everybody is – there isn't anybody who doesn't fit in', or 'We all join up together in one big gang – no cliques or coteries', or 'It doesn't matter where I go, because I don't have to stop and consider whether I'll be welcome, because I know I am'. In this accepting climate, individuals can take stock of themselves and find the courage to undertake what may be quite a radical overhauling of their personal attitudes and values.

Not everyone will put these experiences into words, but the direction of progress matters more than verbalizations, and the important thing is that the process continues, with a snowball effect as group feeling develops, and with an overall increase in safety and comfort. 'No one gets hurt here', and this implicit belief can breed confidence and trust.

Several important points emerge from all this. The first is the balance between the demands of the external world (the syllabus) and the pressing personal concerns of the individuals. Neither must be allowed to rule the roost to the exclusion of the other. It is as bad to have a group that has nothing to do but study itself and its own reactions as to have one rigidly glued to the syllabus.

Secondly, to achieve depth it is not necessary to be sensational. We can compare the non-directive approach to proceeding from the shallow end of a swimming-bath to the deep end. You paddle in the shallows and as confidence increases are prepared to venture further and again further, but still keeping within your depth. If you go too far you know you can get back and so confidence is built up. The choice is with the individual as to how far he will commit himself, and his readiness to proceed is the guiding factor. When he finally reaches the deep end as a confident swimmer he is prepared to stay there and disport himself in it. In the same way, a group whose members have gradually become accustomed to reacting honestly and sincerely among themselves can not only operate confidently at considerable depth but also provide support for each other as each in turn ventures further towards self-knowledge and self-acceptance. The insight of one is shared and made available to the others: whether they use it or not is up to them, depending on their state of readiness. This seems to be psychologically more valuable than exposing all to the same outside stimulus. It is working from within outwards, rather than, as is more common, from the outside inwards. From time to time I have been struck by hearing an excellent lecture, and marvelled at the amount of deep and difficult material encompassed in it, and compared it with our own slow fumblings which seem so ordinary and simple as hardly to be worth having – but then somehow and almost unnoticed, we do in our own way achieve depth and get there in the end: and when we get there it is real and lasting.

This leads to a third point, the distinction between depth (of material) and involvement (of individuals). The material of a lecture may be very deep (as distinct from difficult), but still remain external to its hearers who are themselves uninvolved. A subsequent discussion in the common-room may be an altogether slighter affair, and yet, because the students are really giving themselves to it, it may mean more to them than the preceding lecture.

This notion of involvement will be a most useful one when we turn, now, to discuss the relationship between productiveness and learning, and group feeling.

Certain experiences are more likely than others to result in learning and growth. Generally, the more we involve ourselves in a situation the more we learn. Notice that the approach here is one of self-involvement, not of memorization. . . . Because of this involvement and commitment, we see things differently, develop new skills and attitudes, and are changed by the process in a number of ways. We have learned by *not* focusing on learning as such: it came as an incidental result of our efforts and activities (Lindgren, 1969, p. 31).

Lindgren speaks of memorization where I speak of 'learning out of the top of the head', and the important point is its relative superficiality compared with the approach of self-involvement. There is a certain unreality about the former – it has come from outside, it has been memorized and reproduced on all the right occasions, but it does not seem to matter much, or to be applied when it comes to the crunch. The simple discussion in the common-room, because it touches people where they really are and gains responses from them that are genuine, is more likely to reflect their concern and involvement than is the lecture that sparked it off. In their informal discussions among themselves students are trying out ideas, testing their compatibility and coherence, and working out what *they* really think. Informal companionship plays a great part in the (real) learning of students, and when we see why this should be so, we are then in a better position to tap this valuable source and harness it in the *official* approaches that the college or university uses to help the students learn. To help the students learn: in the last resort it depends on the student himself what he learns, for while you can take a horse to water, you cannot make him drink. Learning is like eating in that it is not just swallowing a lot of external pabulum, it has also to be digested and incorporated. I have elsewhere (Cleugh, 1962, chapter 4) written in detail of the value of discussion, and of the mechanisms by which a lecturer can utilize this natural (unofficial) approach to learning into his (official) syllabus. Done well, official discussions can be as stimulating, concerned, and sincere as unofficial ones: done badly, they can be as frustrating a waste of time as anything else done badly. Running discussions is not easier but far harder than lecturing, and it is not enough to collect together a hotch-potch of students and let them rip, or talk stiltedly, or stay in embarrassed silence.

Let us look now at the features of the common-room discussion that made it valuable. No one was under pressure; all were working at their own level: they were talking honestly: they were not afraid to admit ignorance or doubt: the members of this small self-chosen group were personally compatible with each other: they were trying to fit the jigsaw of their experience into a coherent pattern.

It is evident that these features of the self-organized group cannot be reproduced in an official tutorial situation without considerable effort, and even then not wholly. The group is probably larger, it may not be particularly compatible to begin with, and above all the presence of a tutor raises complications of attitudes to authority, desire to perform well, to do the 'right' thing, and not to expose one's ignorance – all these militate against the sincere expression of ideas which are probably felt to be too callow to be worth producing. There is considerable group expectation that the tutor will take over, and implicitly pressure is put on him to accept the most responsible role. He himself feels he has to prove himself, to gain the respect of his students by being omniscient, so that he is unconsciously only too ready to collude with the students in this way, and retain himself as the final authority. This is so, even if he is not personally 'authoritarian' in the pejorative meaning of the term (if he is, then all the more so), and because of his natural desire to teach, he may not leave the students free enough to learn.

The real tasks of the group leader are to avoid getting pushed into this false position, to let the students do the work, and to provide support and acceptance. However unobtrusive he is his presence makes the occasion 'official' and his tacit approval is expected. This means that he will be discredited if in sober fact the discussion is an awful waste of time, and this is right, because he does have a genuine responsibility even though he tries to diffuse it throughout the group, so that they feel as involved as they do in their self-chosen group. I have earlier sketched out the stages that the group passes through on its way to involvement, having once decided that it can trust the tutor, and that it is safe to express doubts, anxieties, and ignorance in front of him. The presence of the tutor works both ways – the official occasion is harder to get off the ground in the first instance than the unofficial one for reasons already stated, but once take-off is reached his presence can be valuable. His presence is as it were a tacit endorsement of the validity, not so much of the ideas that are expressed, but of the process of search. In effect it is as if he is saying: 'Your struggle to clarify your minds, to express your uncertainties honestly instead of papering over the cracks with a glib know-all superficial bright-ness, is well worth-while and I am confident that you can do it.' By ranging himself on the side of the students he denies the need for a quick summary consensus, and although individual students may be straggled out at all points on the way, each one is able to feel happy with the point he has reached because it is what *he* can cope with. Put differently, this approach postulates, and underwrites, the competence of the students; whereas the traditional starting-point through lecturing underlines the students' ignorance and helplessness. Group discussion that is well done, therefore, is basically encouraging to morale. (It hardly needs to be said that a badly conducted discussion is destructive of morale.)

An interesting point is that the acceptance of and respect for individual differences, which this approach implies, not only improves individual morale (which might be expected) but group morale as well. Let us see why this should be so. A more confident and soundly based attitude in individuals helps them to look with less defensiveness on their neighbours, and a generally more tolerant and accepting climate is thereby produced. The omnis-cient neighbour who has admitted that he is not always sure has gained rather than lost the respect of his colleagues as a result: there is more reality and less pretence in contacts among the group.

During the last few pages I have been writing from the standpoint of a tutor who believes in a non-directive approach as suggested by Rogers, but it is very important to be clear about the differences between non-direction and *laissez-faire*.

'Anything goes' is not the motto of non-direction but of *laissez-faire*. *Laissez-faire* will allow shoddiness and insincerity to pass: non-direction challenges them. A tutor in charge of a discussion group who was completely passive would *not* be conveying an attitude of acceptance, of respect for the students' opinions, of ranging himself on the side of the students – it is far more likely that the message received by the students would be that he was fundamentally uninterested in and careless of their progress. Similarly, a group of children who are allowed to do what they like are prone to interpret this as meaning that adults don't mind what they do because they do not care about them – the absence of prohibitions can be seen as an absence of affection. Adolescents who discuss how they would bring up their own children frequently react sharply against the wrong sort of so-called permissiveness in terms that show they are implicitly equating the absence of sanctions against misconduct with the absence of love – although they phrase it in terms of sanctions and prohibitions, it is probably the lack of positive guidance that is most resented.

So we come back to the need to avoid both the over-direction of authoritarianism, which has a corresponding backlash of resentment and the anarchy of *laissez-faire*, which has a backlash of uncertainty and insecurity. Non-direction is more positive than either, because it entails setting people free to become that which they have it in them to be, to realize their potentialities, to learn, and to grow. It is essentially a forward-looking philosophy with an emphasis always on development, but a development that has come from within, not a sort of forced change imposed from outside that is liable to drop away when the circumstances change. One test of the effectiveness of an education is how far it persists –

it has even been said that 'education is what remains when every-thing one has learnt has been forgotten' (this is of course using 'learnt' in the sense of memorizing, learning by heart, not in the more fundamental sense of learning, which is incorporation and growth). Over a period of time the trappings are lost and what is essential remains – not the facts and figures, but the attitudes of mind. Do people believe in what they are doing, or is their attitude basically cynical? Do they really know what they know (what I have called starting from a steady centre) or are they intellectually rootless and so at the mercy of fads and fashions? I am suggesting that this non-directive approach is valuable because it keeps people within their depth, intellectual and emotional, and while not hurrying growth, encourages it. People proceed at their own pace without being harried, but since the feeling of the group is for-ward, they are heartened to go on. There is all the world of difference between reassurance which often is not reassuring at all, because superficial ('of course you are all right' when you know you aren't – a mere denial of difficulties does not help anyone) and genuine encouragement. It is the latter, the genuine sort, which is involved here, for it is deeply heartening and confidence-building to be a member of an accepting group, and the individual is freed to go forward. The whole of 'In Retrospect' is relevant here, and especially the reference to the 'deep affection' for each other felt in the group.

One of the most important aspects of all this is its open-ended-ness. Creative thinking does not flourish in a tight system, and it tends to be divergent rather than convergent. Obviously it is only an occasional individual who can reach new and original conclu-sions, but a discovery that has been made many times before can still be a genuine new insight for the pupil or student and result in a feeling of mastery that is deeply satisfying. In so far as he is encouraged by the example of the group to have faith in himself and his own abilities instead of the passive acceptance of (and often inner rebellion against) outside authority, the student's develop-ment has been forwarded. We may at this point return to Jean, the conscientious but hollow student of a preceding chapter. Jean had always worked hard, but with no joy; an excellent example of an other-directed personality. When she relaxed her striving for an unattainable perfection it was a great relief to no longer feel guilty because she could not reach it. She was not doing *the* (perfect) best, but she was doing *her* best, and felt more comfortable within herself. The energies that had been wasted in driving herself on to polish and repolish, always feeling that nothing could be good *enough*, could now be more profitably employed. When she became less demanding of herself, and more relaxed, her work became less tight and more her own. As English was her main subject, the greater freedom of her work to her great surprise brought her improved marks – though the quantity had diminished, the quality had improved, being both lighter and more thoughtful (if this is not a contradiction!) – lighter in that it was less deadly dull, more thoughtful in that it reflected more of her own experience and feelings. She became more willing to chance her arm and write on a subject that interested her without following up every conceivable reference and putting them down in a chaotic catalogue that lost sight of the wood in the trees. Her own ideas began to come in, and this was satisfying. She still remained other-directed in the sense of being conscientiously aware of the expectations of her tutors, but was taking much more of the responsibility for her work herself, and finding satisfaction in the process. Less driven, she was working more successfully. Tutors often mistakenly feel that they should keep on driving their students, but in fact more work and of better quality is often achieved by taking the pressure off. Driving is basically counterproductive.

Jean's example could be paralleled by that of many others. The change from an other-directed attitude towards a more inner-directed one is by many experienced as a release, an accession of energy and confidence, and results in greater productiveness. The niggling fears that slow down effort lose their sway and the individual moves forward in something like top gear. This itself is a heartening experience, and immediately rewarding, and so its repetition is sought – a virtuous spiral has been set going, in which improved output leads to increased confidence and vice versa. It is less important to work long hours than to work effectively, and for effective learning one needs a proper level of difficulty, a manageable level of complexity, a basic confidence in one's power to achieve, and adequate motivation. Group discussion appears slow, but this is helpful to an individual if he realizes that the right starting-point for him is one where he is comfortable and does not feel that he is being rushed off his feet out of his depth: its slowness allows for the consolidation of things that have been learned and also allows them to be fitted into a coherent and meaningful pattern (seeing the shape of the wood): his confidence is maintained: his motivation tends to move from the external orientation of wait-for-the-teacher, fear-of-failure, in the direction of greater spontaneity, interest, and personal involvement. In this movement the other members of the group act as helpful mediators, drawing out ideas, considering them, acting as chopping-boards, providing new aspects for consideration, but (if group morale is good) always with a friendly and helpful background which is at the same time acceptant yet stimulating, secure yet questing, and above all confidence-building.

So it is that an individual passing through the stages described at the beginning of this chapter finds himself being underpinned by the group and also being part of the underpinning of others – the reciprocity of the relationship is helpful, for as he takes so also he has something to give. His contributions are welcomed and accepted and this encourages him to contribute further. As a contributing member of the group, he has worth, he has an accepted place, and from this place he is ready to proceed, making sorties as it were outwards. His discoveries and insights he brings back, as trophies for the group, and there they are considered and 'chewed over' (note the relevance of the metaphor), just as are also the ideas of others. The cross-fertilization of ideas is stimulating, and again he continues, with increasing productiveness. The search is one that will not end, not in one person's lifetime, not ever, but in the meantime the group has helped its members through involvement to learn, to grow, and to go on experiencing.

And as well as their individual productiveness, their productiveness *as a group* is vital. This depends on their cohesion: there is a world of difference between a group supposedly working as a team but rent by feuds and one that is friendly, supportive, and purposeful. A united group with high morale performs its task to the satisfaction of its members and the benefit of society, and its hallmarks are gaiety, creativity, and productiveness.

References

Anderson, H. H., Brewer, J. E., and Reed, M. F., 1946. *Studies of Teachers' Classroom Personalities*, Vols. 2 and 3. Stanford, Calif.: Stanford University Press.

Batten, T. R., 1967. *The Non-Directive Approach in Group and Community Work*. London: Oxford University Press.

Cleugh, M. F., 1957. *The Slow Learner*. London: Methuen.

—— 1962. *Educating Older People*. London: Tavistock

—— 1968. 'Against Interpretation'. *Forum*, **10**, 3.

Farley, R., 1960. *Secondary Modern Discipline*. London: Black.

Gardner, D. E. M., and Cass, E., 1965. *The Role of the Teacher in the Infant and Nursery School*. London: Oxford University Press.

Hargreaves, D. H., 1967. *Social Relationships in a Secondary School*. London: Routledge and Kegan Paul.

Holt, J., 1964. *How Children Fail*. London: Pitman.

Jackson, B., 1964. *Streaming*. London: Routledge and Kegan Paul.

Leighton, A. H., 1946. *The Governing of Men*. Princeton University Press.

Lindgren, H. C., 1969. *The Psychology of College Success*. New York: Wiley.

Loughmiller, C., 1965. *Wilderness Road*. Austin, Texas: Hogg Foundation for Mental Health.

Marshall, S., 1963. *An Experiment in Education*. London: Cambridge University Press.

NSSE (National Society for Study of Education), 1950. 49th Yearbook. Part II. *Education of Exceptional Children*. Chicago: University of Chicago Press.

OSS (Office of Strategic Services), 1948. *The Assessment of Men*. New York: Rinehart & Co.

Partridge, J., 1966. *Middle School*. London: Gollancz.

'Miss Read', 1955. *Village School*. London: Michael Joseph.

Rogers, C. R., 1951. *Client-centered Therapy*. Boston: Houghton Mifflin.

—— 1961. *On Becoming a Person*. Boston: Houghton Mifflin.

Sherif, M., and Sherif, C. W. 1953. *Groups in Harmony and Tension*. New York: Harper.

Staines, J. W., 1958. 'The Self Picture as a Factor in the Classroom.' *British Journal of Educational Psychology*, **28**, 97.

Webb, L., 1967. *Children with Special Needs in the Infant School*. London: Smythe.

Index